MONASTIC

Maureen F. McCabe, OCSO

Inside the Psalms
Reflections for Novices

MONASTIC WISDOM SERIES

Patrick Hart, OCSO, General Editor

Advisory Board

Michael Casey, OCSO	Terrence Kardong, OSB
Lawrence S. Cunningham	Kathleen Norris
Bonnie Thurston	Miriam Pollard, OCSO

MW1 Cassian and the Fathers:
Initiation into the Monastic Tradition
Thomas Merton, OCSO

MW2 Secret of the Heart: Spiritual Being
Jean-Marie Howe, OCSO

MW3 Inside the Psalms: Reflections for Novices
Maureen F. McCabe, OCSO

MW4 Thomas Merton: Prophet of Renewal
John Eudes Bamberger, OCSO

MW5 Centered on Christ: A Guide to Monastic Profession
Augustine Roberts, OCSO

MONASTIC WISDOM SERIES: NUMBER THREE

Inside the Psalms
Reflections for Novices

by

Maureen F. McCabe, OCSO

Foreword by
Bernardo Bonowitz, OCSO

CISTERCIAN PUBLICATIONS

Cistercian Publications

*The work of Cistercian Publications is made possible in part by support from
Western Michigan University to The Institute of Cistercian Studies.*

Library of Congress Cataloging-in-Publication Data

McCabe, Maureen F.
  Inside the Psalms : reflections for novices / by Maureen F. McCabe ;
foreword by Bernardo Bonowitz.
      p.   cm. — (Monastic wisdom series ; no. 3)
  Summary: "Reflections on the Psalms which invite contemplation
while also being exegetically sound; originally intended for those in
discernment about a monastic commitment"—Provided by publisher.
  Includes bibliographical references and index.
  ISBN-13: 978-0-87907-009-0 (pbk. : alk. paper)
  ISBN-10: 0-87907-009-9 (pbk. : alk. paper)
  1. Bible. O.T. Psalms—Meditations.   2. Monastic and religious life.
I. Title.   II. Series.

BS1430.54.M35   2005
223'.206—dc22

                                                                    2005008824

Printed in the United States of America

In gratitude to Sister Gertrude Ballew,
my novice director,
who opened this door to me.

CONTENTS

FOREWORD

Saint Paul was a person more accustomed to order than to ask, and to order "with authority" rather than as a suppliant. But as an old man in prison, grace and suffering got through to him, and he learned to make this beautiful and humble request to his friend Philemon: "Refresh my heart" (v. 20). If your heart has been taught to make this same plea, and with the same spirit, thanks be to God: You have come to the right book. Open it up and drink.

I say "drink" because Sister Maureen's book is essentially water, sister water. The reader will soon discover (and enjoy) flashes of fire, feel himself reassured by its rootedness in the earth of human reality and more than once find himself borne aloft on the wind of its trinitarian mysticism. But above all this book is kindly water. Water to drink and water to drown in, water to wash in, and most surprisingly, water to stand on. As Sister Maureen writes: "Out of the depths I cry to you . . . the depths. I sink down and down and down only to discover that I am floating on the words of one who knew deeper depths than I."

The fountainhead of all these waters is the human soul of Christ, revealed to us in the psalms. The Cistercian writers of the twelfth and thirteenth centuries found their supreme motive for wonderment and joy in Jesus, masterpiece of humanity. His human mind thought the thoughts of God, his human heart felt the love, grief, and exultation of God, and all his person reflected—incarnated—the beauty of God. Sister Maureen tells us right at the beginning that the grace of the psalms—prayed, meditated, and lived—is that they communicate to us this inner reality of Christ. Communicate *unitively:* for as we penetrate deeper and deeper into these ancient prayers, our own minds take on the tonality and radiance of Christ's. Recently some Brazilian friends affirmed to me what first seemed medieval allegory but might be modern fact (who knows?): the flamingo, found in the northeast of the country, is born white, but because it feeds voraciously, constantly, and exclusively on shrimp, gradually becomes shrimp-colored, dawn-colored. Sister Maureen promises us that whoever is radically and perseveringly faithful to the psalms will likewise change his innermost skin and become Christ from the inside. Anyone who loves Christ or who desires to love him (in particular Cistercian novices to whom this book is especially addressed) will feel his heart leap at this promise and find his hand grasping for his psalter.

Several years ago, Sister Maureen gave a course to our community on the Cistercian Mothers—mystics such as Gertrud, Beatrice, Lutgard, and Mechtild—referred to in this text. At the end of the course, I wanted to show her at least one of the great natural glories of Brazil. We went to see the waterfalls at Foz de Iguacu and while there found time to visit the *Parque das Aves* (Bird Park). Sister Maureen was most entranced by the loris—a gray bird, perkily silent when left alone, but who, when talked to, displays an astounding repertory of songs, sounds, peeps and trills. Maureen egged him on for the better part of a half-hour, laughing all the while, and succeeded in making him reveal more and more of himself. The Psalms talk to Sister Maureen as she talked to the loris, and out of her Cistercian silence and simplicity—out of her heart—she responds with profound, lovely, true—and perky—music. I am happy to think that as soon as you turn this page you will begin to hear her sing.

Bernardo Bonowitz, ocso
Nossa Senhora do Novo Mundo,
Brasil

INSIDE THE PSALMS

PREFACE:
THE FORMATIVE POWER
OF THE PSALMS

To say I had the good fortune would be an understatement, so I will be precise. I had the incredible fortune, the blessing and the joy to have been strongly encouraged in my initial formation to memorize the psalms and to pray them frequently. That I never made it to Psalm 150 and that I forgot much of what I memorized make not the slightest difference. What matters is that I dove into deep waters and that I was swept irretrievably into the rapids of those Spirit-songs. As a result they have been the intimate friends of my ongoing formation, providing in each situation, no matter how unexpected, much of what was truly needed: light, medicine, patience, stamina, peace.

To go on singing the psalms in our hearts after we have been immersed in them during the Divine Office; after we have prayerfully pondered one or other of them in *lectio divina* is, of course, a natural process. Still it requires something of a deliberate effort and discipline to nurture this process. It means, among other things, befriending psalms for which we have no immediate affinity, opening ourselves to strange words and alien concepts, waiting patiently with a psalm until the Spirit bears us away into its deep heart.

Saint Jerome writes that the key to the mansion of the Psalter is the Holy Spirit but that each room of the mansion, each psalm, has likewise its proper key.[1] It is precisely in the search for these keys that I have been touched most deeply by

---

[1] *The Homilies of Saint Jerome* (Washington, D.C.: The Catholic University of America Press, 1964) 1:3.

the power of the psalms to form a life in Christ. There are valuable aids to understanding the Psalter: *lectio*, study, a bit of basic Hebrew if possible; but it is only when one discovers the thoughts of Christ, his dispositions, and his very prayer welling up in one's heart through the medium of a psalm that one has discovered its key. His joy here, his deep agony there, his questioning, his trust, his wonder, and his praise, indeed, countless movements of his heart are preserved for us in these prayers which were his prayers. It is a way of endless discovery, a way of entering into the mind of Christ, and, consequently, of allowing our minds and prayers to be shaped by his.

For one who is struggling against evil thoughts while they are yet young, these prayers of Christ, these precious distillations of all Scripture, are an incomparable strength and source of healing. Be it acedia or anxiety or whatever, I know that my mind cannot long withstand the force of a psalm verse repeated faithfully and earnestly. These tiny, secret, divine words cause an inner sun to rise and rivers of peace to flow.

There are, of course, those devastating moments when one's very meaning seems knocked out from under oneself. No easy solutions here, it's true. But there are blessedly hard psalms: My only friend is darkness . . . Out of the depths I cry to you . . . the depths. I sink down and down and down only to discover that I am floating on the words of one who knew deeper depths than I and who prayed these words before me. In his depths I wait more than watchmen for the morning.

I could go on, but why not journey together now into the interior.

PSALM 1: *MEDITATIO* DAY AND NIGHT

Happy are those
who do not follow the advice of the wicked,
or take the path that sinners tread,
or sit in the seat of scoffers;
but their delight is in the law of the Lord,
and on his law they meditate day and night.
They are like trees planted by streams of water,
which yield their fruit in its season,
and their leaves do not wither.
In all that they do, they prosper.
The wicked are not so,
but are like chaff that the wind drives away.
Therefore the wicked will not stand in the judgment,
nor sinners in the congregation of the righteous;
for the Lord watches over the way of the righteous,
but the way of the wicked will perish.

Beginnings are often so tiny, yet so significant. Psalm 1, the door to the mansion of the Psalter, is one such beginning. I stand before this door and listen to the chanting within, chanting that haunts and draws me; yet when I open the door my experience is that of the bride, an experience of absence rather than the expected presence:

My hands dripped with myrrh,
my fingers with liquid myrrh,
upon the handles of the bolt.
I opened to my beloved,
but my beloved had turned and was gone.[1]

---

[1] Song 5:5-6.

This is the crucial moment. If you really want to enter into the secret of a psalm, you must be willing to seek, to call, and to hold your ground when the enchantment has gone. You must accept the ordinary, obscure, and laborious way in: repetition without exhilaration. He who could not be found as you pondered the sinners and scoffers of verse 1, may mysteriously rise up and reveal himself as the happy man of verse 2, the one who delights in God's words day and night; for it will often be a single verse or phrase, faithfully repeated, that will illumine the entire psalm for you. Suddenly Jesus is present, drawing you inside, and you understand experientially what Bernard describes, "When with eager minds we examine his rulings, the decrees from his own mouth; when we meditate on his law day and night, let us be assured that the Bridegroom is present, and that he speaks his message of happiness to us lest our trials should prove more than we can bear. . . . Happy the man who has the word for an inseparable companion who is always accessible, whose delightful conversation is an unceasing pleasure."[2]

Happy the one who has discovered this secret. She avoids loitering at all costs because a delightful and all absorbing conversation awaits her if she will but learn the art of *meditatio*: "On his law she meditates day and night." *Meditatio* is Saint Jerome's translation of the Hebrew word for "murmuring," a form of utterance that involves a heartfelt repetition of God's words, be it the psalms or other scriptural texts, savoring them over and over, bearing them about, and gradually being borne by them. It is the primary duty of the beginner whom Saint Benedict sends to the place where the novices eat, sleep, and engage in *meditatio*.[3] Each morning after the Night Office they apply themselves anew to a *lectio* in which *meditatio* is of signal importance,[4] that process whereby what they learn by heart remains in the heart to instruct, console, and strengthen them; or, to use an image describing the *lectio* of Saint Gertrud, they fill

---

[2] Bernard of Clairvaux, *On the Song of Songs*. Cistercian Fathers series 7 (Kalamazoo: Cistercian Publications, 1976) 137, 140.

[3] See RB 58:5.

[4] See RB 8:3.

the basket of their hearts to the very top with inspiring texts so as always to have one at hand to appease their hunger.[5]

Benedict, who drew so frequently from the Wisdom tradition, incarnates Psalm 1 in his Rule. The word is the monk's food, day and night. In the liturgy we listen to it and respond to and with it; in *lectio* we commune with it and bring it with us throughout the day in the form of *meditatio*. As disciples we listen to it in the teaching and directives of the Abbess; as sisters we listen for it in one another in a spirit of mutual reverence, obedience, and caring. In silent prayer we become one with it. Happy are we if we live and breathe and become rooted in God's word for we will grow like trees near living waters.

[5] Gertrud of Helfta, *The Herald of God's Loving-Kindness*. Cistercian Fathers series 35 (Kalamazoo: Cistercian Publications, 1991) 39.

PSALM 2: COMMUNION IN CHRIST

Why do the nations conspire,
and the peoples plot in vain?
The kings of the earth set themselves,
and the rulers take counsel together,
against the Lord and his anointed, saying,
"Let us burst their bonds asunder,
and cast their cords from us."
He who sits in the heavens laughs:
the Lord has them in derision.
Then he will speak to them in his wrath,
and terrify them in his fury, saying,
"I have set my king on Zion, my holy hill."
I will tell of the decree of the Lord:
He said to me, "You are my son;
today I have begotten you.
Ask of me and I will make the nations your heritage,
and the ends of the earth your possession.
You shall break them with a rod of iron,
and dash them in pieces like a potter's vessel."
Now therefore, O kings, be wise:
be warned, O rulers of the earth.
Serve the Lord with fear,
with trembling kiss his feet,
or he will be angry, and you will perish in the way;
for his wrath is quickly kindled.
Happy are all who take refuge in him.

If Psalm 1 is the door to the mansion of the Psalter, then the eagerness of the Holy Spirit to lead us to his most beautiful room is evident, for immediately before us is Psalm 2, the door

of the Messiah. Even before opening it, we can hear the corona-
tion music within. When we enter we bow down our lives forever before the Father's word to Jesus: "You are my Son."

I cannot read this verse without the image of the young
Jesus praying in the hills or in the synagogue of Nazareth loom-
ing up in my heart. How did he pray this psalm? How did he
hear this decree? What did he experience in the depths of his
being when he heard and sang and meditated those words that
were an essential part of the rite of adoption of the Messiah by
God: "I will tell of the decree of the Lord: He said to me, 'You
are my son, today I have begotten you. Ask of me and I will
make . . . the ends of the earth your possession.'"

Here the eyes of our heart turn toward the mystery of divine
filiation in the Trinity, now incarnate in Jesus of Nazareth. When
we look at him we see the Father and touch the holy communion in which they dwell. We are even privy to their sacred dialogue as we hear the Father say, "Ask of me." And for what did
he ask, knowing as he did the total seriousness with which the
Father made this promise, a promise Jesus echoed many times:

> Ask and it will be given you . . . [1]

> Very truly, I tell you, if you ask anything of the Father in
> my name, he will give it to you. Until now you have not
> asked for anything in my name. Ask and you will receive,
> so that your joy may be complete.[2]

He asked for the ends of the earth; he asked that we, too, might
be sons and daughters in himself, the Son; that we might be one
even as he and the Father are one.

Communion is the ultimate goal, the ultimate desire, the
ultimate mystery. It is the deepest vocation of the Church: "For
as long as all of us who are sons of God and comprise one family in Christ, remain in communion with one another in mutual
charity and in one praise of the most Holy Trinity, we are re-
sponding to the deepest vocation of the Church and partaking
in a foretaste of the liturgy of consummate glory."[3]

[1] Luke 11:9.
[2] John 16:23-24.
[3] Constitution *Lumen Gentium*, 7:51.

We cenobites are a tangible sign of communion. Our very name reveals that we are born of that Jerusalem Church which sought to be of one heart and one mind, having everything in common[4] (*koinos bios*, Greek for common life; *coenobitarum*, Latin for the same). We have our roots as well in the *Koinonia* of Pachomius, the first cenobites, monks who recognized their identity as partnership in Christ, Communion. We are meant to live what we are called. Our Cistercian father, Baldwin of Forde, describes it with theological depth and beauty:

> As the only-begotten Son of God lives with God the Father in the unity of the Holy Spirit . . . so we too, as adopted sons, live under God the Father in the unity of the Holy Spirit, and it is in this Spirit that we cry, "Abba, Father." We do not, of course, say this in the same way as the only-begotten Son. He is at the right hand of the Father and equal to him in all things . . . Our cry certainly comes from far away, but yet, in a certain way, there is a similarity. The unity which is brought about in us by the charity of God is preserved in the bond of peace through the grace of our Lord Jesus Christ. He who makes two to be one is himself our peace. . . . What exactly is this peace which we have been given by Christ, the peace which preserves unity of spirit in its bond? It is the mutual charity with which we love one other, and it remains intact provided we all say the same thing and there are no divisions among us. . . . In this charity, unity of spirit is preserved as the bond of peace. This, therefore, is the law of the common life: unity of spirit in the charity of God, the bond of peace in the mutual and unfailing charity of all the brethren, the sharing of all goods which should be shared, and the total rejection of any idea of personal ownership in the way of life of holy religion. Our hope is that this may be found in us, as in those who have but one heart, one soul, and all things in common.[5]

Something wonderful begins to happen in our prayer as we grow in this communion of love and this love of communion. We

---

4 Acts 4:32.

5 Baldwin of Forde, *Spiritual Tractates*. Cistercian Fathers series 41 (Kalamazoo: Cistercian Publications, 1986) 175–176.

begin to ask as Jesus did, with joyful confidence, with great expectations, and with our lives. We begin to care for one another, for the Church, for the whole human race as Jesus cares, he who lives forever to intercede for us. Our Sister Maria Gabriella is a good teacher in this way of prayer that flows from communion and moves toward full communion, a prayer which involves conversion of heart as well as desire and confidence. In her own words, "Now I understand that the glory of God and being a victim does not consist in doing great things but in the total sacrifice of my 'ego.' Pray for me that I might understand more and more the great gift of the cross so that I might put it to good use from now on for myself and for everyone."[6]

"For everyone." Is that too much for a Father who has promised to give us the ends of the earth in Jesus?

---

[6] Martha Driscoll, *A Silent Herald of Unity: The Life of Blessed Maria Gabriella Sagheddu*. Cistercian Studies series 119 (Kalamazoo: Cistercian Publications, 1990) 93.

PSALM 4: THE SECRET JOY

Answer me when I call, O God of my right!
You gave me room when I was in distress.
Be gracious to me, and hear my prayer.
How long, you people, shall my honor suffer shame?
How long will you love vain words, and seek after lies?
But know that the Lord has set apart the faithful for himself;
the Lord hears when I call to him.
When you are disturbed, do not sin;
ponder it on your beds, and be silent.
Offer right sacrifices,
and put your trust in the Lord.
There are many who say,
"O that we might see some good!
Let the light of your face shine on us, O Lord!"
You have put gladness in my heart
more than when their grain and wine abound.
I will both lie down and sleep in peace;
for you alone, O Lord, make me lie down in safety.

Every night before sleeping we sing the psalm of the secret joy. We carry it in our hearts down the quiet, sunlit cloisters of summer, down the starlit cloisters of winter. We lie down with it and its words become seeds of grace. Psalm 4 is a psalm of confidence, that is, a lament in which the confidence element of the structure so expands in the psalmist's heart that it becomes a type in itself. Yet, precisely because the trust of these psalms arises in situations where it is hard to trust, they retain their deepest significance when one's actual distress remains close to consciousness.

12

This is quite evident in Psalm 4 whose doorway is very narrow. The trust which flows from it has been refined by the fire of the hemmed in situation, something built into our lives by our vow of stability. As we face work that we dread or a difficult relationship or perhaps the pain of our prayer, our solitude or our obvious limitations, there is no place to go but in and deep. Whatever it is that hems us in makes us cry out:

> Answer me when I call, O God of my right!
> You gave me room when I was in distress (literally, "narrowness").

In the heart of this fire which burns up all our supports, we intimately confront a deeper dimension and we experience as did Paul that God is teaching us to rely not on ourselves but on him who raises the dead to life;[1] even more, that he is mysteriously inviting us to know him both as our only certainty and as wide open space. Then the psalmist's conviction can become our own: "You alone, Lord, make me lie down in safety" and again, "Know that the Lord has set apart the faithful for himself."

We are set apart for God, consecrated for an undivided love of Jesus Christ, called to a "special grace of intimacy" with him.[2] This is the secret joy. There is another joy, of course: that of feeling fulfilled, on top of the world, the "plenty of grain and wine inebriation." But the secret joy is God's gift to the poor: "You have put gladness in my heart more than when their grain and wine abound." In it we celebrate the simple truth that in all insufficiency, he suffices.

If it takes time to recognize this as joy, don't be concerned, for one acquires a taste for it over time. It is much like hidden manna, a food that sustains us we know not how, a food so unfamiliar that we do not immediately delight in it. We may experience it more as a space that God opens to us when we have no way out, an emptiness full of hope. At the end of each Cistercian day we breathe free in that space and pray, "I will both lie down and sleep in peace."

---

[1] See 2 Cor 1:8-9.
[2] John Paul II, Apostolic Exhortation, *Vita Consecrata* (Rome: 1996) number 16.

Resting upon our beds in this peace, we "worthily and quietly commemorate the Lord" to ourselves[3] and say with Gilbert of Hoyland, "Good is the confinement of this little bed which knows how to welcome only its Beloved, that is Christ alone. Indeed there is a narrowness which knows how to welcome him only."[4] Yes, in the secret places of the heart he sets us apart, makes us lonely, that he alone might enter in to share with us his jubilation.

[3] *The Rule of the Master.* Cistercian Studies series 6 (Kalamazoo: Cistercian Publications, 1977) 224.

[4] Gilbert of Hoyland, *Sermons on the Song of Songs.* Cistercian Fathers series 14 (Kalamazoo: Cistercian Publications, 1978) 56.

PSALM 8:
THE TIME OF YOUR VISITATION

O Lord, our Sovereign,
how majestic is your name in all the earth!
You have set your glory above the heavens.
Out of the mouths of babes and infants
you have founded a bulwark because of your foes,
to silence the enemy and the avenger.
When I look at your heavens, the work of your fingers,
the moon and the stars that you have established;
what are human beings that you are mindful of them,
mortals that you care for them?
Yet you have made them a little lower than God,
and crowned them with glory and honor.
You have given them dominion over the works of your hands;
you have put all things under their feet,
all sheep and oxen, and also the beasts of the field,
the birds of the air, and the fish of the sea,
whatever passes along the paths of the seas.
O Lord, our Sovereign, how majestic is your name in all
        the earth!

Who are we that God cares for us or, as it may also be rendered, that he visits us? Most holy Traveler on our rough roads, how will you visit me? Will it be as you visited Sarah or Hannah or the Hebrews in Egypt, working something new and beyond my power in your coming? Setting me free? Watching over my growth? Or will you visit me as you visited Job, pushing me to my limits, destroying my peace, until I cry out with him:

> What are human beings, that you make so much of them,
>   that you set your mind on them,
>   visit them every morning,
>   test them every moment?[1]

This rich Hebrew word, *visit*, which combines the various senses of *visit, look upon, investigate, inspect, test, be concerned about, care for,* is used for both visits of judgment and visits of mercy. The common element in all God's visits is that he enters our history to enact salvation.

He enters our history: visits always have a historical character, that is, they are unrepeatable. I will never pass this precise spot again—and neither will he.

To enact salvation: a visit which is a blessing for one becomes a blessing for the many; a visit which is a punishment becomes a purification.

The visitations of the Old Testament came to their completion when the loving kindness of the heart of our God visited us like the dawn from on high in Jesus, he who rides into the personal history of each of us, waiting and knocking at the door of our freedom: "As he came near and saw the city, he wept over it, saying, 'If you, even you, had only recognized on this day the things that make for peace! But now they are hidden from your eyes. Indeed, the days will come upon you, when your enemies will set up ramparts around you and surround you . . . because you did not recognize the time of your visitation from God.'"[2]

How to know the critical time? Jesus, he who visits us, is also one who was visited, and from his own experience he teaches us how to tell time, how to detect the *kairos* in the *chronos,* the sound of our hour that has come or has not come, our unique hour, within the ceaseless flow of day and night, summer and winter. As Son of Man he was for a little while made lower than the angels, entering into the suffering of death, experiencing its darkest depths; but in the tomb a door opened to that visit that is the source of all visitations: the Resurrection.

---

[1] Job 7:17-18.
[2] Luke 19:41-44.

Psalm 8 stands as a testimony to this moment in which the Father visits Jesus with glory and honor and abiding jubilation:

> But we do see Jesus, who for a little while was made lower than the angels, now crowned with glory and honor because of the suffering of death, so that by the grace of God he might taste death for every one.[3]

Our personal visitations are a participation in this meeting of Father and Son, revealing depths of ourselves hitherto unknown, depths recognizable by the peace and certainty of the Spirit's voice within. For our Cistercian fathers and mothers these personal visits were a very significant dimension of the mystical life and they described them as deeply interior, certain, unrepeatable, brief, rare, and powerful enough to change the course of one's life forever. Since they are experienced as part of one's personal salvation history, the descriptions of them often indicate time, place, and setting as, for example, this early and important visit to Gertrud:

> But you who say "Here I am!" before you are summoned, anticipated that day by forestalling me, unworthy as I was, in the blessings of sweetness. On the vigil of that feast (the Annunciation), because it was a Sunday, chapter took place at Lauds. I cannot find the words to describe how you, the Dayspring from on high, then visited me through the depths of your loving-kindness and sweetness. Giver of gifts, give me this gift: may I henceforward offer on the altar of my heart a sacrifice of joy. [4]

More than anything else, these visits signify how precious each human person is to God and what dignity each possesses in being invited to intimacy with the Word.

Psalm 8, then, captures perhaps more than any other the exuberant optimism in Cistercian spirituality and anthropology. Through, with, and in Jesus we are made little less than God, are crowned with glory and honor, given dominion over

---

[3] Heb 2:9.
[4] Gertrud, *The Herald,* CF 35:104.

all the earth and, beyond our wildest dreams, given hearts capable not only of receiving divine visits but of gradually being transformed by them into permanent dwelling places:

> Next, a thing very sweet to experience, as it is very rare; such is the courtesy of the Word, such the tenderness of the Father towards the well disposed, well ordered soul—itself the gift of the Father and the work of the Son—that they honor with their own presence the one whom they have fore-ordained and prepared for themselves, and not only do they come to him, but they make their dwelling place with him.[5]

[5] Bernard, *SC*, CF 40:28.

THE PSALMS AND REMEMBERING

Turn, O Lord, save my life;
deliver me for the sake of your steadfast love.
For in death there is no remembrance of you;
in Sheol who can give you praise?

Psalm 6:4-5

The first step of humility is the clear eye, the reciprocal gaze, the abiding memory of the Beloved. It is living always toward the face of the One who seeks us:

> O Lord, you have searched me and known me,
> You know when I sit down and when I rise up;
> You discern my thoughts from afar,
> You search out my path. . . .[1]

God is relentless in his search for us. At every hour and in every place he calls, "Show me your face." He would have us know as did Hagar in the desert, Abraham on the mountain, that he is the God who sees and foresees; that he is the God with eyes of fire purifying the heart by his tender glance and truthful gaze: "God searches the heart and the loins."[2]

The Divine Searcher asks us to turn to him wherever and however he may show himself; to return his gaze; to be perpetually watchful, even in the night: "I slept but my heart was awake."[3] To open one's eyes to the deifying light calls for an ascesis of attentiveness.

---

[1] Ps 139:1-3; RB 7:16.
[2] Ps 7:9; RB 7:14.
[3] Song 5:2.

One could say that prayer begins here in this responsiveness to the gaze of God. Although we must make many about-faces day after day to meet his gaze and to flee the oblivion to which we are so prone, every step toward purity of thought, intention, heart, toward purity of the inner eye, leads us more surely to that sanctuary called memory, a sanctuary created in us by God precisely so that we could meet him there, *Memoria Dei.*

What is it to remember God? To remember him is not simply a recollection of him in his past deeds because those mercies shape us to this day. To remember him is to enter into his presence in the varied ways that he makes himself present within and among us. It is to know that forgetfulness of God is death: "In death there is no remembrance of you."[4] It is to say to God what he says to us: "I will never forget you."[5]

This practice of remembering was very dear to our fathers and mothers in whose anthropology memory was well developed. William of Saint Thierry has some beautiful descriptions of this faculty of which the following are only a taste:

> God established, as it were, in the apse, the summit of the soul, the power of memory. It is here that the Father has his couch, at that secret point where resides the latent remembrance of his goodness and power . . . the most deeply graven trait of his image, that which evokes all the other faculties and enables us to make ourselves like him.[6]

> This is your purpose—to feed the lover's understanding with the knowledge of your truth, out of the abundance of your sweetness, and to consecrate unto yourself his memory in which you ever have your couch with delight.[7]

Saint Benedict himself gives us this practice in the first degree of humility when he advises that we flee mindlessness by

[4] Ps 6:5.

[5] Isa 49:15.

[6] William of Saint Thierry, *On the Nature of the Soul,* as quoted in Roger DeGanck, *Beatrice of Nazareth in Her Context.* Cistercian Studies series 121 (Kalamazoo: Cistercian Publications, 1991) 128.

[7] William of Saint Thierry, *Exposition on the Song of Songs.* Cistercian Fathers series 6 (Spencer, Massachusetts: Cistercian Publications, 1970) 45.

keeping a psalm verse continually on the lips.[8] This practice involves not an absence of thought but a strict selectivity of thought, a great quieting of one's own thoughts in order to be in touch with the thoughts of God which he himself inspired in the hearts of the psalmists and continues to inspire in the hearts of all who pray the psalms. It is not simply a matter of saying sacred words, but of feeling with them and moving with them into the long, silent pauses that are an inherent part of them, the pauses that are the threshold of the presence of God. This experience is particularly powerful when the psalm verse is a question, for when the Spirit of God questions, the only sufficient answer will be a divine one. Deep calls unto deep. And the power of the questions themselves sustain us in a silence full of hope:

How long, O Lord? Will you forget me forever?[9]

O God, who is like you?[10]

Where can I go from your Spirit?[11]

Whom have I in heaven but you?[12]

How can young people keep their way pure?[13]

What shall I return to the Lord for all his bounty to me?[14]

Why are you cast down, O my soul, and why are you disquieted within me?[15]

In time, the spaces of interior silence become more prolonged and the words needed to sustain them less frequent. God opens a path to continual mindfulness.

---

[8] See RB 7:18.
[9] Ps 13:1.
[10] Ps 70:19.
[11] Ps 139:7.
[12] Ps 73:25.
[13] Ps 119:9.
[14] Ps 116:12.
[15] Ps 42:5, 11.

PSALM 15: EXAMEN

O Lord, who shall sojourn in your tent?
Who may dwell on your holy hill?
Those who walk blamelessly, and do what is right,
and speak the truth from their heart;
who do not slander with their tongue,
and do no evil to their friends,
nor take up a reproach against their neighbors;
in whose eyes the wicked are despised,
but who honor those who fear the Lord;
who stand by their oath even to their hurt;
who do not lend money at interest,
and do not take a bribe against the innocent.
Those who do these things shall never be moved.

Who shall sojourn in your tent? In Hebrew the word sojourn denotes dwelling in another's land, being a guest or an alien resident. Who, then, shall be God's guests? This beautiful little psalm goes on to explain that they shall who live like God, adopting the customs of his kingdom, embracing them, as Saint Benedict instructs, with a sense of urgency: "If we wish to dwell in the tent of that kingdom, we must run to it by good deeds or we shall never reach it."[1]

Since we are called each day to confess our sins to God in prayer,[2] called to live in continual conversion, this is a good psalm for one's daily examen, focusing as it does on thoughts, words and deeds. Let us proceed with the Gospel as our guide as well as the invaluable teachings of our monastic fathers and mothers

[1] RB Prologue:22.
[2] RB 4:57; *Constitutions and Statues, O.C.S.O.* (Rome, 1990) C. 15:2.

on what is traditionally called the active life, that is, the strenuous labor involved in weeding out vices and planting Christlike habits. Beatrice of Nazareth's first mode of love may prove particularly helpful to us here: "Such a soul often seriously scrutinizes what it is, what it should be, what it possesses, and what is lacking to its desire. With all its diligence, with great longing and all possible ingenuity it strives to beware and avoid whatever can impede or harm it in this matter. Its heart never rests from inquiring and entreating and learning and drawing to itself and retaining whatever can help or bring the soul toward love."[3]

THOUGHTS: Those who speak the truth from their heart

In biblical usage the heart is the seat of reflection and choice, a person's very center. Our words and our deeds flow from the thoughts of our heart, and hence these must be guarded with care.

Have I taken every thought captive to obey Christ?[4]

Have I dashed my wayward thoughts while they were yet young against Christ the Rock?[5]

Have I yielded my thoughts to whatever is true, honorable, just, pure, lovely, gracious, excellent, and worthy of praise?[6]

Did I take seriously the three steps of truth described by Saint Bernard?

   a) Did I look for truth in myself by judging myself truly?
   b) Did I look for truth in my neighbors by a love that united me with them so closely that I felt their good and ill as if it were my own?
   c) Did I look for truth in itself by my efforts to pray with a pure heart?[7]

[3] *The Life of Beatrice of Nazareth*, translated and annotated by Roger De Ganck, Cistercian Fathers series 50 (Kalamazoo: Cistercian Publications, 1991) 293.
[4] 2 Cor 10:5.
[5] RB 4:50.
[6] Phil 4:8.
[7] See Bernard, *Liber de gradibus humilitatis et superbiae, Treatises II.* Cistercian Fathers series 13 (Washington, D.C.: Cistercian Publications, 1974) 34–35.

Do I have a mind ready to put a wrong interpretation on everything?[8]

WORDS: *Those who do not slander . . . nor take up a reproach against their neighbors . . . who stand by their oath even to their hurt.*

When I spoke of others today, did I keep in mind that life and death are in the power of the tongue?[9]

Were my words long considered and cleansed in my heart before they issued from my mouth?[10]

Did I watch others in order to imitate or to disparage?[11]

Did I go apart with another or others to gossip?[12]

Did my words flow from genuine love for the person spoken of?[13]

Because of envy did I discourage, disparage, or misrepresent another?[14]

Did I immediately rush to retaliate?[15]

Did I, under the guise of administering correction, pierce with sharp and searing words one for whom Christ was pleased to be crucified?[16]

Did I mutter and murmur complaints?[17]

Did I keep my word despite inconveniences, setbacks, or unexpected pressures?

---

[8] Guerric of Igny, *Liturgical Sermons*. Cistercian Fathers series 32 (Spencer, Massachusetts: Cistercian Publications, 1971) 22.
[9] Prov 18:21; RB 6:5.
[10] *RM*, CS 6:129.
[11] Bernard, *SC*, CF 7:44.
[12] Bernard, *SC*, CF 7:44.
[13] See Bernard, *SC*, CF 7:45.
[14] Bernard, *SC*, CF 31:29.
[15] Bernard, *SC*, CF 7:107.
[16] Bernard, *SC*, CF 7:107.
[17] Bernard, *SC*, CF 7:107.

DEEDS: Those who walk blamelessly, and do what is right . . . and do not take a bribe against the innocent.

Have I looked into Jesus as a mirror for my deeds as John of Forde suggests:
My harsh dealings in light of his gentleness?
My impatience in light of his patience?
My impurity in light of his innocence?
My lack of compassion in light of his compassion?[18]

Is love set in order in my relationships as William describes:

If I was asked to lead, did I do so with solicitude?
If I was subject, did I do so with humility?

Did I encounter those with whom I live cheerfully?
Did I go out of my way for others, putting their concerns before my own?[19]

As Bernard describes:
Was I obedient to my superiors, obliging to my companions, and kind to my subjects?[20]

Did I prove myself a sister among sisters, a brother among brothers, by taking Guerric's advice to hold to the royal road of truth that lies between the two vices of silly amiability on the one hand and proud aloofness on the other?[21]

Did I heed the teaching of Gertrud to plead with Jesus on behalf of others with bold confidence? To offer myself through Jesus, with him, and in him in the eucharistic sacrifice with absolute trust in his desire to send his loving kindness flowing through me to the other members of his body?[22]

---

[18] John of Forde, *On the Song of Songs*. Cistercian Fathers series 43 (Kalamazoo: Cistercian Publications, 1982) 77–78.

[19] William of Saint Thierry, *The Nature and Dignity of Love*. Cistercian Fathers series 30 (Kalamazoo: Cistercian Publications, 1981) 81.

[20] Bernard, *SC*, CF 7:33.

[21] Guerric, *Sermo in festo sancti Benedicti*, CF 32:21.

[22] Gertrud, *Herald*, CF 63: see 79–81, 198–201.

As we take on the mind of Christ through a daily conversion of our thoughts, words, and deeds, we begin to taste the peace of the kingdom toward which we are journeying and to experience within ourselves a kind of interior stamina springing from deeper reliance on the voice of the Spirit within. Such persons, the psalmist assures us, are deeply grounded and shall never be moved! In the words of Mechtild of Magdeburg:

> His eyes in my eyes,
> His heart in my heart,
> His soul in my soul,
> Enclosed and at peace.[23]

---

[23] Mary Jeremy Finnegan, *The Women of Helfta* (Athens: The University of Georgia Press, 1991) 18.

PSALM 16: THE JOY OF JESUS RISEN

Protect me, O God, for in you I take refuge.
I say to the Lord, "You are my Lord;
I have no good apart from you."
As for the holy ones in the land,
they are the noble, in whom is all my delight.
Those who choose another god multiply their sorrows;
their drink offerings of blood I will not pour out
or take their names upon my lips.
The Lord is my chosen portion and my cup;
you hold my lot.
The boundary lines have fallen for me in pleasant places;
I have a goodly heritage.
I bless the Lord who gives me counsel;
in the night also my heart instructs me.
I keep the Lord always before me;
because he is at my right hand, I shall not be moved.
Therefore my heart is glad, and my soul rejoices;
my body also rests secure.
For you do not give me up to Sheol,
or let your faithful one see the Pit.
You show me the path of life.
In your presence there is fullness of joy;
in your right hand are pleasures forevermore.

If you pray any psalm during Paschaltide, let it be this one. Enter into the joy of Jesus who shines like a candle, springs about, trembles with delight: all the varied senses of the joy words used here. The first generation of Christians, enlightened by the Spirit, seized upon Psalm 16 as a witness to the death and resurrection of Christ, and it has remained ever since an open door to those who love and believe in him.

Before he died Jesus spoke of how joyful we should be for him in his return to the Father. How true, yet how far we may find ourselves from such a disposition; so far perhaps that I wonder if Saint Bernard's four steps of love may not be paralleled by four steps of joy. I recall vividly my first Easter in the monastery when I, a somewhat woebegone postulant of ten months, tried unsuccessfully to feel cheerful as we recited the beautiful canticle of Guerric of Igny at Vespers:

> Now, my brethren, what witness to Christ's love does the joy of your hearts give you? I venture to judge, and rightly as you will see, that if you have ever loved Jesus alive or dead or risen from the dead, your heart rejoices within you today. As the tidings of his resurrection resound and re-echo again and again through the Church you will say to yourselves: "They have told me that Jesus my God is still alive. On hearing it my spirit, which was asleep through weariness, languishing through tepidity, disheartened through timidity, has revived." For the joyful voice of this happy message raises even from death those buried deep in sin . . . By this token you may clearly know that your soul lives again fully in Christ if it echoes this sentiment: "It is enough for me that Jesus is still alive." How faithful and worthy of a friend of Jesus is that voice, how pure that act of love which says: "It is enough for me that Jesus is still alive."[1]

My interior response was, "It's not enough for me! I can't even say I want it to be enough for me because my other wants and needs are clamoring so loudly. But at least I can say from the bottom of my heart that I want to want to want it to be enough for me that Jesus lives." Four steps removed from the pure joy that can say, "If he wishes, then, let him take no account of me. It is enough for me that he still lives even if he only lives for himself."[2]

[1] Guerric, *Sermo in die paschae,* CF 32:84.
[2] Guerric, *Pasc.,* CF 32:84.

Ten Easters later life had changed. It is as if seeds were secretly planted and growing during the long night of those years, I know not how. One Easter morning I awakened to discover a verse of Psalm 16 in my heart and since then it has not ceased to be my Paschaltide psalm: "In your presence there is fullness of joy." Twenty years later another verse unfolded, "I bless the Lord who gives me counsel; in the night also my heart instructs me." Thirty years later it is simply, "And so my heart is glad."

When we remain still and allow the Lord to be the gardener of our hearts, when we gratefully receive the Holy Spirit Jesus breathes upon us whether in wind or storm or gentle breeze, then his words begin to bear fruits of unselfish love in our hearts. In such love we finally taste the joy Guerric was describing: "The more humble it is, the more lasting it is; the more severe it is, the truer it is; the holier it is, the sweeter it is. O blessed Jesus, how different is the joy with which you comfort those who turn their backs on that deceitful and deceiving joy. How much is your steadfast love better than life, for a day in your courts is better than a thousand elsewhere."[3]

---

[3] Guerric, *Sermo in die sancto pentecostes*, CF 32:112.

PSALM 18: PRIMEVAL WATERS

I love you, O Lord, my strength.
The Lord is my rock, my fortress, and my deliverer,
my God, my rock in whom I take refuge,
my shield, and the horn of my salvation, my stronghold.
I call upon the Lord, who is worthy to be praised,
so I shall be saved from my enemies.
The cords of death encompassed me;
the torrents of perdition assailed me;
the cords of Sheol entangled me;
the snares of death confronted me.
In my distress I called upon the Lord;
to my God I cried for help.
From his temple he heard my voice,
and my cry to him reached his ears.
Then the earth reeled and rocked;
the foundations also of the mountains trembled
and quaked, because he was angry.
Smoke went up from his nostrils,
and devouring fire from his mouth;
glowing coals flamed forth from him.
He bowed the heavens, and came down;
thick darkness was under his feet.
He rode on a cherub, and flew;
he came swiftly upon the wings of the wind.
He made darkness his covering around him,
his canopy thick clouds dark with water.
Out of the brightness before him
there broke through his clouds hailstones and coals of fire.
The Lord also thundered in the heavens,

and the Most High uttered his voice.
And he sent out his arrows, and scattered them;
he flashed forth lightnings, and routed them.
Then the channels of the sea were seen,
and the foundations of the world were laid bare
at your rebuke, O Lord,
at the blast of the breath of your nostrils.
He reached down from on high, he took me;
he drew me out of mighty waters.
He delivered me from my strong enemy,
and from those who hated me;
for they were too mighty for me.
They confronted me in the day of my calamity;
but the Lord was my support.
He brought me out into a broad place;
he delivered me, because he delighted in me.
The Lord rewarded me according to my righteousness;
according to the cleanness of my hands he recompensed me.
For I have kept the ways of the Lord,
and have not wickedly departed from my God.
For all his ordinances were before me,
and his statutes I did not put away from me.
I was blameless before him,
and I kept myself from guilt.
Therefore the Lord has recompensed me according to my
*   righteousness,*
according to the cleanness of my hands in his sight.
With the loyal you show yourself loyal;
with the blameless you show yourself blameless;
with the pure you show yourself pure;
and with the crooked you show yourself perverse.
For you deliver a humble people,
but the haughty eyes you bring down.
It is you who light my lamp;
the Lord, my God, lights up my darkness.
By you I can crush a troop,
and by my God I can leap over a wall.
This God—his way is perfect;

the promise of the Lord proves true;
he is a shield for all who take refuge in him.
For who is God except the Lord?
And who is a rock besides our God?—
The God who girded me with strength,
and made my way safe.
He made my feet like the feet of a deer,
and set me secure on the heights.
He trains my hands for war,
so that my arms can bend a bow of bronze.
You have given me the shield of your salvation,
and your right hand has supported me;
your help has made me great.
You gave me a wide place for my steps under me,
and my feet did not slip.
I pursued my enemies and overtook them;
and did not turn back until they were consumed.
I struck them down, so that they were not able to rise;
they fell under my feet.
For you girded me with strength for the battle;
you made my assailants sink under me.
You made my enemies turn their backs to me,
and those who hated me I destroyed.
They cried for help, but there was no one to save them;
they cried to the Lord, but he did not answer them.
I beat them fine, like dust before the wind;
I cast them out like the mire of the streets.
You delivered me from strife with the peoples;
you made me head of the nations;
people whom I had not known served me.
As soon as they heard of me they obeyed me;
foreigners came cringing to me.
Foreigners lost heart,
and came trembling out of their strongholds.
The Lord lives! Blessed be my rock,
and exalted be the God of my salvation,
the God who gave me vengeance
and subdued peoples under me;

who delivered me from my enemies;
indeed, you exalted me above my adversaries;
you delivered me from the violent.
For this I will extol you, O Lord, among the nations,
and sing praises to your name.
Great triumphs he gives to his king,
and shows steadfast love to his anointed,
to David and his descendants forever.

As I began to memorize the psalms, I wondered how I would fare with Psalm 18. I didn't want to skip any, but perhaps I could make an exception of that big lump of strangeness, much like a dinosaur, that comes so early on. Most of all it was that nose. How could I think of God with a nose at all, let alone a nose like that—huge, red, breathing smoke? What disposition in Jesus could possibly open the door of this psalm to me? But I was determined to make friends and a friend I found, a wise and ancient one.

This psalm and several others can provide a surprising amount of consolation when life falls apart and personal chaos reigns, particularly by means of their watery depths imagery. These immense waters are so blinding, so lacking in solidity and foothold, that there is nothing to do but to sink in helplessness and cry out:

The cords of death encompassed me,
the torrents of perdition assailed me;
the cords of Sheol entangled me.
The snares of death confronted me.
In my distress I called upon the Lord;
to my God I cried for help . . .
Then the channels of the sea were seen,
and the foundations of the world were laid bare,
at your rebuke, O Lord,
at the blast of the breath of your nostrils.
He reached from on high, he took me,
he drew me out of many waters.

And in another psalm:

Save me, O God!
For the waters have risen to my neck.
I sink in deep mire,
where there is no foothold;
I have come into deep waters,
and the flood sweeps over me.
I am weary with my crying;
my throat is parched.
My eyes grow dim
with waiting for my God.[1]

Such moments are the really decisive ones in the making of a monk, the impossible moments, the moments when we experience the limits of our own efforts and discover within ourselves vast areas as yet untransformed by the light of Christ; primeval waters over which the Spirit hovers anew. Then the channels of our sea are seen and the foundations of our inner world are laid bare. As we sink to the bottom, to ground zero, we begin to learn truly that we have nothing to lean on, neither ourselves nor others nor created securities. Our hearts cry out, "Who is a rock but our God?"

We get a glimpse of such moments in Saint Benedicts's developments of the fourth, fifth, sixth, and seventh steps of humility as well as in his treatment of impossible things. Let's look at the seventh step here, the step in which the monk experiences with the most heartfelt inner conviction who he or she is before God, not in comparison with others, but simply in the truth of one's interior poverty before the most pure God. This step resembles a lighthouse in a treacherous sea. Through one's very groundedness in the Lord and the light of conviction that shines from within, one is able to gaze without wavering upon all that rages against this quiet, still center, all the inclinations toward envy and resentment, anger, possessiveness, and so much else that still have their high tides.

These seem often to be moments overshadowed by the cross, moments of personal failure or discouragement, loss or injustice. If we look to the Crucified, he who entered into the

---

[1] Ps 69:1-3.

watery depths before us and for us, we may hear him ask, "Are you able to be baptized with the baptism with which I am baptized?" By this question he invites us to join him in his total immersion in our misery so that united with him we may experience the Father "drawing us out of many waters." In the words of John of Forde: "His passion was close at hand, and he was on the point of going down into that vast ocean of his suffering, in which Pharaoh with all his chariots and horsemen had to be drowned. . . . He is my head and I am a part of his body, however small. So I can never know any wound or bruise or grief which he does not suffer with me, which he, in a word, does not heal. Such is the very close partnership, the covenant, the union, the kiss of peace between us."[2]

These moments of abandonment that we share with Christ are too sacred to be of our own making. In fact one must never anticipate one's hour (such was the test of authentic martyrdom in the early Church), but rather receive it from the hand of the Father at the ordained time. I have come to recognize these moments of total immersion by a certain sign: when events conspire to cast me into the watery depths and, fighting for all I'm worth to keep afloat, I do so, then I can say with the psalmist,

> He made my feet like hind's feet,
> and set me secure on the heights.
> He trains my hands for war,
> so that my arms can bend a bow of bronze.

But when I struggle with all my might to no avail, then I know it's time to abandon myself to the difficult situation with all its confusion and misery, time to settle down for a good while to the dark side of the paschal mystery. Eventually I will be drawn out of the waters and will discover some of God's secret work in my soul. Yet even during the experience, I know one thing for sure: it is the Lord and together we sink!

[2] John of Forde, *SC*, CF 39:188.

PSALM 23: *QUIES*

The Lord is my shepherd, I shall not want.
He makes me lie down in green pastures;
he leads me beside still waters;
he restores my soul.
He leads me in right paths for his name's sake.
Even though I walk through the darkest valley,
I fear no evil;
for you are with me;
your rod and your staff—they comfort me.
You prepare a table before me
in the presence of my enemies;
you anoint my head with oil;
my cup overflows.
Surely goodness and mercy shall follow me
all the days of my life,
and I shall dwell in the house of the Lord
my whole life long.

Jesus is himself the door of Psalm 23, door of the sheepfold and of the green pastures and restful waters beyond. As we pass by, he, our good Shepherd, calls us by name and speaks words of irresistible beauty and comfort: "Come to me, all you that are weary and are carrying heavy burdens, and I will give you rest. Take my yoke upon you, and learn from me; for I am gentle and humble in heart, and you will find rest for your souls."[1] This psalm, so filled, even in the shadow of death, even in the presence of enemies, with quiet confidence in the one

---

[1] Matt 11:28-29.

who gives us soul-rest (*quies* or *requies* in Latin), can lead us to a profound experience of the peace the world cannot give.

This theme of rest, *quies,* is one of the most beautiful in Sacred Scripture. We can hear it in the Song of Songs: "Tell me, you whom my heart loves, where do you rest your flock at noonday?";[2] we can hear it in the prophets who give eloquent witness to the human heart's thirst for rest, no one of them more consistently than Isaiah; and its most beautiful fruit seems to be the much loved Good Shepherd psalm. Let me take a moment to present Isaiah's thoughts for they will lead us immediately inside Psalm 23 where his spirit seems so perfectly distilled, especially in the words, "He leads me beside waters of rest; he restores (returns) my soul," an echo of "In returning and in rest you shall be saved."[3] Here and in countless other instances we discover the truth of Saint Athanasius' teaching that the Psalter is a garden which, besides its own special fruit, grows also some of those of all the other books.[4]

Isaiah was a quiet man with a quiet heart who lived in the midst of an unquiet people. The quietness which he loved was an inner quality born of goodness and trust:

> The effect of righteousness will be peace,
> and the result of righteousness, quietness and trust forever.[5]

> In returning and rest shall you be saved,
> in quietness and in trust shall be your strength.[6]

Returning, rest, trust, peace, quietness, all of these words are interrelated in Isaiah and point to the gift of rest God offers his people: "This is rest; give rest to the weary."[7] The path to rest is a difficult one, however. It demands a return to childlike simplicity which, in concrete terms, requires not building up defenses, non-manipulativeness, an obedience full of faith and a quietness

---

[2] Song 1:7.
[3] Isa 30:15.
[4] *The Letter of Saint Athanasius to Marcellinus on the Interpretation of the Psalms, St. Athanasius on the Incarnation* (London: A. R. Mowbray & Co. Ltd., 1953) 98.
[5] Isa 32:17.
[6] Isa 30:15.
[7] Isa 28:12.

that is not passivity but total trust in a God who means what he says. In short, this path demands the strength of weakness or, in Isaiah's terms, "leaning upon the Holy One of Israel in truth."[8] Only such trust can bring about inner stillness and only inner stillness can withstand the fears, real and imaginary, that make havoc of our minds. Has anyone ever said this more beautifully than Isaiah: "Those of steadfast mind you keep in peace—in peace because they trust in you?"[9]

This trust which creates rest, this rest which strengthens trust, is something more than silence. Or rather, it is silence at its deepest. It is that silence which is "a putting aside, a renouncing of all schemes, desires, inclinations and thoughts . . . which prevent us from expressing ourselves wholly before God."[10] It is the third depth of the call received by Arsenius: *Fuge, tace, quiesce*— "flee, be silent, pray always"[11] or, as I like to translate, "flee, be silent, rest in God." It is the dream that burned in the hearts of our fathers as they eagerly headed for the desert-place of Citeaux: "We decree, therefore, that the place where you have chosen to dwell for monastic quiet *(quiete)* is to be safe and free from all mortal molestation";[12] and again, "take care that . . . those who love the desert live together there in quiet" *(conquiescant)*.[13]

I think that each of us Cistercians can recount our own *"fuge, tace, quiesce"* journey with all its particulars. The flight element generally entails a difficult period of leaving behind, letting go, grieving, facing culture shock, and gradually internalizing the values of the monastic desert. Silence plays an important part in this transition, greatly aiding the process but also posing its own set of challenges, since by means of silence so much interior stuff begins to surface and to demand attention and appropriate action. During our first few years in the monastery we

[8] Isa 10:20.
[9] Isa 26:3.
[10] Andre Louf, *Teach Us to Pray* (Chicago: Franciscan Herald Press, 1975) 43–44.
[11] *The Sayings of the Desert Fathers*, translated by Benedicta Ward. Cistercians Studies series 59 (Kalamazoo: Cistercian Publications, 1975) 8.
[12] *Exordium Parvum* 14:5 as in Chrysogonus Waddell, *Narrative and Legislative Texts from Early Citeaux* (Citeaux: Commentarii cistercienses, 1999) 428.
[13] *Exordium* 6:6; Waddell, 423.

find ourselves very active in the sense of the "active life" described earlier. In my own experience, the beginnings of *quies* came toward the end of the Novitiate during our yearly retreat. I can clearly recall that it was a summer retreat with so many opportunities for walks in the fields and for quiet reflection by the brook hidden deep in the woods. At the time I must have been living with Psalm 23, this much loved Shepherd psalm that everyone seems to know by heart from childhood. One day as I stood in the woods in the utter stillness of high noon, I realized that I, too, interiorly, had become utterly still and that it hadn't happened in a day. One verse of the psalm became a door for me into understanding what God had been doing in my soul during this novitiate, and it filled me with a sense of homecoming:

> He leads me beside still waters;
> he restores my soul.

To receive one's soul from the hands of Christ, restored, is to experience God breathing life within us as in a new Eden, a new beginning; to hear the Good Shepherd call one's name, one's unique and irreplaceable name, is to want for nothing; to know the rest of green pastures and still waters is to enter into the interior quiet that is not the tranquility of order but the surrender of unconditional love.

PSALM 25: CISTERCIAN ADVENT

To you, O Lord, I lift up my soul.
O my God, in you I trust;
do not let me be put to shame;
do not let my enemies exult over me.
Do not let those who wait for you be put to shame;
let them be ashamed who are wantonly treacherous.
Make me to know your ways, O Lord;
teach me your paths.
Lead me in your truth, and teach me,
for you are the God of my salvation;
for you I wait all day long.
Be mindful of your mercy, O Lord, and of your steadfast love,
for they have been from of old.
Do not remember the sins of my youth or my transgressions;
according to your steadfast love remember me,
for your goodness' sake, O Lord!
Good and upright is the Lord;
therefore he instructs sinners in the way.
He leads the humble in what is right,
and teaches the humble his way.
All the paths of the Lord are steadfast love and faithfulness,
for those who keep his covenant and decrees.
For your name's sake, O Lord,
pardon my guilt for it is great.
Who are they that fear the Lord?
He will teach them the way they should choose.
They will abide in prosperity,
and their children shall possess the land.
The friendship of the Lord is for those who fear him,
and he makes his covenant known to them.

My eyes are ever toward the Lord,
for he will pluck my feet out of the net.
Turn to me and be gracious to me,
for I am lonely and afflicted.
Relieve the troubles of my heart,
and bring me out of my distress.
Consider my affliction and my trouble,
and forgive all my sins.
Consider how many are my foes,
and with what violent hatred they hate me.
O guard my life, and deliver me;
do not let me be put to shame, for I take refuge in you.
May integrity and uprightness preserve me,
for I wait for you.
Redeem Israel, O God,
out of all its troubles.

It was Advent when God began to turn Saint Gertrud's heart toward himself in the tender, confident intimacy that is so characteristic of her. She writes, "You began in the Advent before the Epiphany on which I turned twenty-five, by means of a sort of upheaval which disturbed my heart so that all the undisciplined living of my youth began to lose its attraction for me."[1] Advent is an unfailing beginning, the season of fresh hope in each new year of grace, a season so dear to Cistercians and so incomparably lovely.

God himself created this beauty when, at the dawn of our redemption, he looked upon the earth and said, "Let there be Advent: let there be Mary and the consolations of Isaiah; let there be *'Ad Te Levavi'* and the pure heart of John; let there be hymns of longing so ancient that one can stand in choir at first vespers and tremble with the pulsating presence of all humanity aching for its Lord; let there be solemn O's and trips to the woods for evergreens; and for some, as a sign for all, let there be blessed winter to make it very clear that the human heart is cold, longing for warmth; dark, longing for light; barren, longing for birth."

<hr />

[1] Gertrud, *Herald*, CF 35:164.

"*Ad Te Levavi,*" the ancient chant composed of the first few verses of Psalm 25 is Advent's entrance song:

> To you, O Lord, I lift up my soul,
> O my God, in you I trust,
> let me not be put to shame,
> do not let my enemies exult over me.
> Do not let those who wait for you be put to shame.

The melody is full of discreet joy, the fruit of confidence, abandon, peace, and love as Dom Baron, one of our early chant teachers, describes it.[2] The words themselves hold secrets that they disclose gradually to those who live with them. One of the secrets is Mary.

When Mary visited Elizabeth she had just conceived of the Holy Spirit. When she left her to return to Nazareth, she was returning to people to whom she could not explain the great mystery within her and who would very likely not receive her as Elizabeth had. Would misunderstanding result in violence? Would Joseph protect her? Would God give him light? Would God give her words? "*Ad Te Levavi*" is so natural on her lips: "To you I lift up my soul . . . in you I trust; let me not be put to shame." Suddenly she is there with us, this young woman, so vulnerable and so trusting; there with us in the midst of our own upheavals, anxieties, needs, efforts to trust. Mary has so many ways of being present to us, but in Advent we especially experience her as our sister, one who knows our joys and perils from the inside. As we pray this psalm, Mary becomes our companion on the road back to our own Nazareths, making the journey much sweeter by her presence and teaching us how to pray in times of uncertainty: "Make me to know your ways, O Lord; teach me your paths."

I came to know Mary in this way during my first Advent in the monastery when, walking one day in the woods and reading these words, we suddenly stood, interiorly, sister to sister:

> For thou alone of all mankind
> thought gloriously in thy strong mind

[2] Dom L. Baron, *L'Expression du Chant Gregorien* (Plouharnel-Morbihan: Abbaye Sainte-Anne de Kergonan, 1947) 7.

that thou wouldst bring to thy Maker thy maidenhood,
give it, sinless. Not again
will such another come of men
a maiden ring-adorned who will thus send
heaven-homeward with ever pure heart
her bright treasure.[3]

The poem became a mirror for me and the kindest, gentlest invitation to self-knowledge I have ever received. Spontaneously I said, "I am not like you, Mary." We agreed and together we walked home through those winter woods to begin my formation in humble love, a formation whose beginnings are so bound up with Psalm 25:

Lead me in your truth and teach me,
for you are the God of my salvation;
for you I wait all day long . . .
Do not remember the sins of my youth or my transgressions;
according to your steadfast love remember me.
Good and upright is the Lord. . . .
He leads the humble in what is right,
and teaches the humble his way.

If we begin our Advents with her and with this psalm, we will be certain of approaching Bethlehem in her presence also. "Following her, you will never go astray. Asking her help you will never despair. Keeping her in your thoughts, you will never wander away. With your hand in hers, you will never stumble. With her protecting you, you will not be afraid. With her leading you, you will never tire. Her kindness will see you through to the end."[4]

---

[3] Cynewulf, *A Maiden Ring-Adorned*, *The Mary Book* (New York: Sheed and Ward, 1950) 70.

[4] Saint Bernard, *Homelium super Missus est in laudibus virginis matris, Magnificat*. Cistercian Fathers series 18 (Kalamazoo: Cistercian Publications, 1979) 30–31.

PSALM 26: DEFENSELESSNESS

Vindicate me, O Lord,
for I have walked in my integrity,
and I have trusted in the Lord without wavering.
Prove me, O Lord, and try me;
test my heart and mind.
For your steadfast love is before my eyes,
and I walk in faithfulness to you.
I do not sit with the worthless,
nor do I consort with hypocrites;
I hate the company of evildoers,
and will not sit with the wicked.
I wash my hands in innocence,
and go around your altar, O Lord,
singing aloud a song of thanksgiving,
and telling all your wondrous deeds.
O Lord, I love the house in which you dwell,
and the place where your glory abides.
Do not sweep me away with sinners,
nor my life with the bloodthirsty,
those in whose hands are evil devices,
and whose right hands are full of bribes.
But as for me, I walk in my integrity;
redeem me, and be gracious to me.
My foot stands on level ground;
in the great congregation I will bless the Lord.

Psalm 26 is a lament with much protestation of innocence. This attitude is not at all pharisaical, however, for the psalmist is not speaking of innocence at all times and in all ways. He is referring to a particular instance in which he was falsely accused or misunderstood, something to which we can all relate.

The literal sense obviously involves a temple liturgy: "I will go around your altar." In post-exilic Israel the liturgy became well organized and people from all over the country could come to the temple for a liturgy of thanksgiving or penitence or, in this case, pleading innocent and seeking acquittal from the Lord through a priest.

Let's reflect on the very first word of the psalm: "Vindicate me," that is, defend me, set things straight, be on my side. If I vindicate myself it is useless. If God does not speak to the heart of the other about me, what I say on my own behalf will not be heard. For those who fear and love and trust God, there can be utter certainty that he will take care of reputation as well as other needs. All of this is related to a certain silence on the part of the one accused, a silence well depicted in another psalm:

> But I am like the deaf, I do not hear;
> like the mute, who cannot speak.
> Truly, I am like one who does not hear,
> and in whose mouth is no retort.
> But it is for you, O Lord, that I wait;
> it is you, O Lord my God, who will answer.[1]

Recall the moments in Jesus' trial when he refused to answer. Treated harshly he, like the Suffering Servant, never opened his mouth. He knew that God would answer for him. I believe that part of the charism of the monastic life is to permit us to enter more deeply into the mystery of Jesus' defenselessness and that the teachings of the Rule, especially the fourth degree of humility, can lead to an experience of Jesus and of ourselves that we might never know otherwise. The quiet mind with which Saint Benedict encourages us to embrace difficulties can sometimes open onto a room we would not choose to enter of ourselves, except that the sight of our brother Jesus, standing in the midst of his accusers with such unthreatened dignity, such quiet trust, such vulnerability and pain, invites us to taste from within our own hearts his self-emptying for our sakes.

[1] Ps 38:13-15.

Our Cistercian father, John of Forde, speaks very power-fully of Jesus' defenseless silence:

> My Lord Jesus was silent before the scribes and pharisees when they accused him, silent before his judges when they questioned him, silent before those who punished him with torture and crucifixion. Even today, he is silent before the wicked and shameless men who challenge him every day and every hour. If this is so, then plainly that silence of his is full of grace and truth . . . Which of you, dearest brothers, will give his heart to being a loving imitator of this sacred silence? Who will enter that school of hidden philosophy and sit at Jesus's feet? . . . If you truly believe that you have enrolled in this school, you will not consider that you have yet become a philosopher, in the full sense of the word, if your lips refrain from speech when a brother insults you, but the depths of your heart swell with anger over the quarrel. It is not enough for the tongue to maintain a strict silence outwardly, while all the time fury rages within. Make it your ambition, according to the words of the sage, that your lips consider what is pleasing. By earnest prayer and a gentle reply, both in words and kindly action, strive to win the victory, first over your own spirit, and then over the spirit of the one who injures you. Try to lead both together as captives into the kingdom of meekness.[2]

There is really only one way into this kingdom of humble love of our brothers and sisters: with Jesus, in Jesus, through Jesus. It can never be a question of making oneself a victim, but only of surrendering one's entire life to Jesus and allowing him to lead us as he wills. The details of his plan for each of us are unique, but there is a common pattern: becoming like him in his death and sharing his sufferings that we may know the power of his resurrection. Defenseless—that is to be like him.

---

[2] John of Forde, *SC*, CF 39:103, 105–106.

SEEKING GOD'S FACE IN THE PSALMS

One thing I asked of the Lord,
that will I seek after:
to live in the house of the Lord
all the days of my life,
to behold the beauty of the Lord,
and to inquire in his temple.
For he will hide me in his shelter
in the day of trouble;
he will conceal me under the cover of his tent;
he will set me high on a rock.
Now my head is lifted up
above my enemies all around me,
and I will offer in his tent
sacrifices with shouts of joy;
I will sing and make melody to the Lord.
Hear, O Lord, when I cry aloud,
be gracious to me and answer me!
"Come," my heart says, "seek his face!"
Your face, Lord, do I seek.
Do not hide your face from me.

Psalm 27:4-9

There are moments, as rare as they are brief, that evoke divine nostalgia in us, moments when God draws back the veil, so to speak, for a fraction of a second and in that second we are done for. The yearning to see his face is unleashed, a yearning that is sometimes unbearable and at all times unforgettable. Over the years I have found that the psalm verses which capture this yearning have a special attraction for novices.

47

As the deer longs for flowing streams,
so my soul longs for you, O God . . .
When shall I come and behold the face of God?[1]

One thing I asked of the Lord,
that will I seek after:
to live in the house of the Lord
all the days of my life,
to behold the beauty of the Lord,
and to inquire in his temple . . .
"Come," my heart says,
"Seek his face!"
Your face, Lord, do I seek.
Do not hide your face from me.[2]

You hide them in the secret of your face.[3]

Intuitively we know that this is what life is about, seeking God's face; yet how do we seek the face of one we cannot see? The Hebrew here is enlightening for it has more the sense of turning toward (Face me!) than of facial features. Let's look at three dimensions of this major biblical theme as it appears in Scripture in general, as an aid to our encounter with it in the psalms—and in our thirsting souls.

1) Mystical

On rare occasions God showed his face, that is, revealed his presence to his chosen servants drawing them into special intimacy with himself. Moses had a particularly privileged relationship with the Lord, but there are others as well.

Hear my words:
When there are prophets among you,
I the Lord make myself known to them in vision;
I speak to them in dreams.
Not so with my servant Moses;
he is entrusted with all my house.

---

[1] Ps 42:1-2.
[2] Ps 27:4, 8-9.
[3] Ps 31:20 (translation adapted to text).

With him I speak face to face—
clearly, not in riddles;
and he beholds the form of the Lord.[4]

Jacob called the place Peniel, saying,
"For I have seen God face to face, and yet my
life is preserved."[5]

In the year King Uzziah died I saw the Lord sitting on a
throne, high and lofty; and the hem of his robe filled the
temple. Seraphs were in attendance above him; each has
six wings . . . And one called to another and said: "Holy,
holy, holy is the Lord of hosts; the whole earth is full of his
glory." The pivots on the thresholds shook at the voice of
those who called, and the house filled with smoke. And I
said, "Woe is me! For I am lost, for I am a man of unclean
lips, I live among a people of unclean lips; yet my eyes
have seen the King, the Lord of hosts."[6]

In Jesus the search for God's face is fulfilled: "He who sees me
sees the Father."[7]

2) *Liturgical*

The most frequent use of the phrase "seek his face" was a
cultic one and was, therefore, the use that predominated in the
songs of the cult, the psalms. Believers seek the face of God and
find it when they attend the temple. Here the accent is still on
presence but as experienced in communal worship.

Who shall ascend the hill of the Lord?
And who shall stand in his holy place?
Those who have clean hands and pure hearts,
who do not lift up their souls to what is false . . .
Such is the company of those who seek him,
who seek the face of the God of Jacob.[8]

[4] Nm 12:6-8
[5] Gn 32:31
[6] Is 6:1-5
[7] Jn 14:9
[8] Ps 24:3-4, 6

> As the deer longs for flowing streams,
> so my soul longs for you, O God.
> My soul thirsts for God, for the living God.
> When shall I come and behold the face of God? . . .
> These things I remember as I pour out my soul:
> how I went with the throng,
> and led them in procession to the house of God,
> with glad shouts and songs of thanksgiving,
> a multitude keeping festival.[9]

In worship we are most truly ourselves, caught up together in God, turned toward the Father in Jesus and he toward us. We taste the ultimate meaning of life in these experiences of communion, foreshadowings of the day when all will be one in the union of Father and Son.

3) Moral

Worship overflows into a daily relationship with God where all that we do matters. Psalm 105 calls us to "constantly seek his face,"[10] the face of him who is mindful of his covenant forever and who desires that we keep his statutes and observe his laws. Seeking is truly doing; it is walking in God's commands.

Of all our fathers and mothers, it is William of Saint Thierry who is our foremost teacher in the meaning and application of this phrase, this imperative of the heart. Judging from his devotion to the texts of Scripture that speak of God's face, we could say that "for him the spiritual life might be defined as 'seeking the face of God. . . .' He was convinced that God aids with his countenance him who looks at him. He moves him and excites him. The beauty of the sovereign good draws him who contemplates him."[11]

Although William would have had good reason to apply this phrase in all three of its dimensions, I believe that it is primarily the mystical meeting with God in the depths of the heart that preoccupies him and, secondarily the moral commitments that lead to and flow from such meetings. Among many apt

---

[9] Ps 42:1-2, 4.
[10] Ps 105:4.
[11] William, *Cant*, CF 6:28, note 17.

passages, the following are good illustrations of the interior vision for which he so hungered and thirsted:

> What shall we say of the roe? It has very sharp sight. I have no wish, says the Bride, to be like Adam and hide myself from the face of him who, with approval or censure, sees all things. Nay rather, I seek your countenance, O Lord; my face seeks your face. For you will give keenness to my interior eyes, that I may contemplate you and give attention to myself.[12]

> For the man who is chosen and loved by God is sometimes shown a certain light of God's countenance, just as light that is enclosed in a man's hands appears and is hidden at the will of him who holds it. This is in order that what he is allowed to glimpse for a passing moment may set the soul on fire with longing for full possession of eternal light, the inheritance of full vision of God.[13]

The psalms are key in his development of this mystical meeting of faces, both Psalm 27 as cited above and several others. Again, it is not features as in a vision but presence as in turning toward that is the heart of this experience:

> Forgive me, Lord, forgive my heart's impatience for you; I seek your face, by your own gift I seek your countenance lest you should turn it from me at the last.[14]

> Turn then to me, most Sweet One, that face which once you turned away from holy David; and, as he was troubled, so shall I be consoled. Turn to me that face by which, before you turned it from him, you willed to increase his beauty. Let your right hand and your arm, and the light of your countenance, which gained possession of the land of those Fathers in whom you were well pleased, take possession also of my land.[15]

[12] William, *Cant*, CF 6:148–149.

[13] William of Saint Thierry, *The Golden Epistle*. Cistercian Fathers series 12 (Kalamazoo: Cistercian Publications, 1976) 97.

[14] William of Saint Thierry, *Meditativae orationes On Contemplating God, Prayer, Meditations.* Cistercian Fathers series 3 (Spencer, Massachusetts: Cistercian Publications, 1971) 102.

[15] William, *Med.*, CF 3:136.

This face of God that we seek, his turning toward us, his presence in prayer, his presence all along our journey, aid and transform us. But in order to see we must also be turned toward him. This wonderful word "turn" or "return" reminds us of an essential element in our search for God's face: continual conversion:

> All the ends of the earth shall remember and turn to the Lord.[16]

> I do not wish the sinner to die, says the Lord, but to turn to me and live.[17]

Jesus will speak similarly: "Unless you turn and become like a little child."[18] The sense is not exactly "return" as if to some ideal state, but changing one's position, shifting, turning around to face the face that can save us, delight us, and reveal us to ourselves. Paul will also use the word "turn" in this sense of conversion: "When one turns to the Lord the veil is removed,"[19] the veil symbolizing here the uncomprehending darkness of the mind; the turning signifying that interior shift of the will which allows us to behold the glory of the Lord and, in beholding, to be changed gradually, "from glory to glory into his likeness." This latter is a text precious to our fathers and is, indeed, one of the classic texts of all Christian mysticism.

Face seeks face and, as the heart is purified, face meets face; for though it is true that only hereafter shall we see face to face, we can rejoice even now to behold him as in a mirror dimly. Ours is a simple and joyous mysticism which finds its key in hiddenness and obscurity rather than in Nada, a mysticism in which we see obscurely the one whom we shall someday see with utter clarity, a mysticism in which we spend our days hidden in the mystery of God's face. William testifies to this when he describes Bernard's beginnings at Citeaux:

---

[16] Ps 22:27.
[17] Ezek 18:32.
[18] Matt 18:3.
[19] 2 Cor 3:16.

Up until then almost no one had resorted there for conversion's sake, given its extremely austere style of life and its poverty. Such things, however, scarcely terrify a mind truly seeking God, and so Bernard, setting aside all hesitation and fear, turned his attention to Citeaux, convinced that there he could shrink from notice and be hidden in the hiding place of God's face.[20]

---

[20] William of Saint Thierry, *Bernard of Clairvaux* (Guadalupe Translations, 1989) 1:13.

PSALM 29: GLORY!

O give the Lord you sons of God,
give the Lord glory and power;
give the Lord the glory of his name.
Adore the Lord in his holy court.
The Lord's voice resounding on the waters,
the Lord on the immensity of waters;
the voice of the Lord, full of power,
the voice of the Lord, full of splendour.
The Lord's voice shattering the cedars,
the Lord shatters the cedars of Lebanon;
he makes Lebanon leap like a calf
and Sirion like a young wild-ox.
The Lord's voice flashes flames of fire.
The Lord's voice shaking the wilderness,
the Lord shakes the wilderness of Kadesh;
the Lord's voice rending the oak tree
and stripping the forest bare.
The God of glory thunders.
In his temple they all cry: "Glory!"
The Lord sat enthroned over the flood;
the Lord sits as king for ever.
The Lord will give strength to his people,
the Lord will bless his people with peace.[1]

In this Psalter-mansion the architecture also reveals secrets. Just as in the ancient cathedrals the play of light had a definite theological function grounded in the mystery, "God is light," so too, even the scaffolding of a psalm can give us a glimpse of the

[1] The Grail Psalter.

glory within. Let us, then, approach Psalm 29 more structurally, a psalm very faithful to the pattern of praise psalms, and discover the amazing way Saint Benedict's own efforts to structure a life dedicated to praise parallel it.

This psalm lifts us immediately into monastic motion, that is, into the rhythm of the Divine Office where ceremony and adoration meet and where, in the beauty of worship, we taste most fully who we are: the city of the living God, the communion of saints with innumerable angels in festal gathering. Saint Basil's words are particularly fitting when considering Psalm 29: "A psalm is . . . the voice of the Church . . . the work of angels, a heavenly institution, the spiritual incense."[2]

1) The Call to Praise

> O give the Lord you sons of God,
> give the Lord glory and power;
> give the Lord the glory of his name.
> Adore the Lord in holy attire.

The spirits above, "sons of the gods," and the worshiping community of Israel on earth are called to give glory to God.

The Abbess or a very careful sister calls the community to the Work of God. Each hastens to it at the call, yet with all gravity and decorum. Each is aware that she prays not only with her sisters and brothers but also "in the sight of the angels," the heavenly court of Psalm 29. Thus all clothe themselves in the beauty of holiness, singing praises wisely, humbly and with profound awe.[3]

2) The Motives for Praise

The psalmist develops the motives for praise, here the Lord's power, by describing in image

In the monastic church the psalmody begins. The rise and fall of the chant, the mood evoked by

---

[2] *Saint Basil: Exegetic Homilies* (Washington, D.C.: The Catholic University of America Press, 1963) 153.
[3] See RB 19:4; 47:4.

upon image the glory of the Lord as revealed in a storm. The dominant phrase, "the Lord's voice," is repeated again and again, each time introducing a variation, the variations being the concrete expositions of his power: shatters the cedars, over the waters, divides the flames of fire, sets the wilderness shaking. This circular movement which expresses his glory, each time from a slightly different perspective, has a mantra-like quality, a gradual progression through repetition. This progression, however, finally builds to a point where the worshipers cannot contain themselves. All cry, "Glory!" One word containing all words, all silence, all joy, all praise.

the particular psalm tone joined to the repetition of the same psalms week after week, provide the deep, restful quality whereby the spirit of each abides in God's presence. Yet a gradual progression of understanding and love takes place as the psalms reveal anew the glory of God in creation and especially in his saving deeds. Each psalm reaches a point where words give way and all cry "Glory!" the point at which Benedict says let "Glory be to the Father" be said, all rising reverently as soon as it begins. And it is at Vespers that he provides for a most eloquent song of glory: "My soul glorifies the Lord."[4]

3) Prayer for Blessing

The Lord sits enthroned as king forever.
May the Lord give strength to his people!
May the Lord bless his people with peace!

Finally the eyes of the Israelites turn from the Lord's glory seen in his mighty deeds to the Lord himself, enthroned on high. Their expression of faith in him is at the same time a prayer that he will bless them with peace and strength.

Hymn and psalmody completed, the eyes of each heart in the monastery turn to the Father in heaven as the Lord's Prayer brings the office to a close. To its Father and King the community prays that his kingdom will come with its blessings; that he will grant the strength of daily bread, the peace of forgiveness and freedom from evil.[5]

[4] See RB 9:7; 11:3; 17:8.
[5] See RB 13:12–14.

What are our cries of "Glory!" our continual doxologies to Father, Son, and Holy Spirit if not a taste even now of the glory that is to be revealed in us, the glory with which the sufferings of this present life are not worthy to be compared? One day on a visit before entering, I observed the community at prayer and I knew with a most certain longing that one profound bow at one "Glory be to the Father" at one little hour would be worth anything I would ever have to go through, and after thirty years I am more convinced of this than ever. That is the weight of glory! Guerric of Igny put it this way: "When you are absorbed in his praises with accents of exultation and thanksgiving, he will take you into the unapproachable light in which he dwells, where he feeds, where he lies down at midday. For if the devotion of those who sing psalms or pray has something of that loving curiosity of the disciples who asked: 'Rabbi, where do you dwell?' they deserve, I think, to hear: 'Come and see.'"[6]

---

[6] Guerric of Igny, *Sermo ad excitandam devotionem in psalmodium*, CF 32 (Spencer, Massachusetts: Cistercian Publications, 1971) 215.

PSALM 32: OPENNESS OF HEART

Happy are those whose transgression is forgiven,
whose sin is covered.
Happy are those to whom the Lord imputes no iniquity,
and in whose spirit there is no deceit.
While I kept silence, my body wasted away
through my groaning all day long.
For day and night your hand was heavy upon me;
my strength was dried up as by the heat of summer.
Then I acknowledged my sin to you.
And I did not hide my iniquity;
I said, "I will confess my transgressions to the Lord,"
and you forgave the guilt of my sin.
Therefore let all who are faithful offer prayer to you;
at a time of distress, the rush of mighty waters shall not
*   reach them.*
You are a hiding place for me;
you preserve me from trouble;
you surround me with glad cries of deliverance.
I will instruct you and teach you the way you should go;
I will counsel you with my eye upon you.
Do not be like a horse or a mule, without understanding,
whose temper must be curbed with bit and bridle,
else it will not stay near you.
Many are the torments of the wicked,
but steadfast love surrounds those who trust in the Lord.
Be glad in the Lord and rejoice, O righteous,
and shout for joy, all you upright in heart.

There is a path to truth that cuts through many detours, a
way advised by the monastic fathers and mothers and by our

Father Benedict: the practice of frequently sweeping out the secret corners of the mind by a frank confession of thoughts to one's Abbot or Abbess (and/or to a spiritual guide they entrust us to). The opposite is concealment and its consequence: lethargy of spirit.

> While I kept silence, my body wasted away
> through my groaning all day long.
> For day and night your hand was heavy upon me;
> my strength was dried up as by the heat of summer.

What we want to look at here in light of Psalm 32 is not sacramental confession but manifestation of thoughts as it stands in our tradition. This psalm, cited by Saint Benedict in his fifth step of humility, is full of insight on the movement from interior bondage to freedom, anticipating the words of Jesus, "The truth will make you free."[1]

First we stand before the eyes of another and through him or her make our way known to the Lord. The imagery of Psalm 32 is very helpful in this regard:

> I will instruct you and teach you the way you should go;
> I will counsel you with my eye upon you.

This mutual gaze is as healing as it is painful, for by it we know that we are accepted as we are: "There is one thing you must attend to with total vigilance: that you always open the windows and lattices of your confessions. Through them his kindly gaze may penetrate to your inward life, because his discerning is your learning."[2]

For the monk this is the path to life. As our Holy Father, John Paul II writes:

> A monk's way is not generally marked by personal effort
> alone. He turns to a spiritual father to whom he abandons
> himself with filial trust, in the certainty that God's tender
> and demanding fatherhood is manifested in him . . . The
> East in particular teaches that there are brothers and sisters

[1] John 8:32.
[2] Bernard, *SC*, CF 31:93.

to whom the Spirit has granted the gift of spiritual guidance. They are precious points of reference, for they see
things with the loving gaze with which God looks at us. It
is not a question of renouncing one's own freedom in
order to be looked after by others. It is benefitting from the
knowledge of the heart, which is a true charism, in order
to be helped, gently and firmly, to find the way of truth.[3]

But what of the inevitable limitations in our guides that
sometimes obscure the kindly or enlightened gaze? Fear not,
the Lord sees and he will never betray, indeed, can only bless
your act of humble faith. Once while waiting for my regular
spiritual direction session, I pondered with heavy heart something I had concealed for a long time. It seemed impossible to
speak of it in the present circumstances and equally impossible
to withhold it lest I lose my monastic heart. Recalling the fifth
step of humility, particularly the words, "Confess to the Lord
for he is good, for his mercy endures forever," I drew from them
the strength I needed to open my heart. Upon doing so I did not
receive a particularly significant response, yet I felt free. After
our talk I entered the Church for Vespers and found myself
overwhelmed and completely reassured by the Lord's response. Over and over Jesus sang through his Church, "Confess
to the Lord for he is good, for his mercy endures forever."[4] Yes,
we can count on it; it is in these moments especially that he secretly manifests himself to the one who trusts him, to the one
who believes that when we meet in his name, there he is in our
midst quietly and powerfully.

Secondly, we should speak with candor. Although our afflicted thoughts rather than our sins are the concern of spiritual
guidance, it is the psalmist's refreshing frankness that is our
focus here:

> I acknowledged my sin to you,
> and I did not hide my iniquity;
> I said, "I will confess my transgressions to the Lord,"
> and you forgave the guilt of my sin.

---

[3] John Paul II, Apostolic Letter, *Orientale Lumen* (Rome, 1995) number 13.
[4] RB 7:46 quoting the refrain of Ps 106.

Saint Bernard speaks of candor as one of the seven marks of genuine confession. We own what is ours without concealment or exaggeration, without making it sound better or worse. It is completely personal and not to be compared with another's way. Perhaps we think we cannot identify with Jesus in this psalm, yet the psalmist's candor is an image of Jesus' openness before the Father, of "his ability to come before the Father so naked and so engaged in the act of revealing" as Adrienne Von Speyr puts it.[5]

Finally, we trust in the grace of God which comes to us through our very openness. His grace can take the form of a word from the Spirit through our guide, our *lectio* and/or our silent prayer; or it can be a wordless interior movement—a greater freedom or peace or sense of safety; a conversion from a difficult habit, a movement of genuine sorrow, or deeper kindness toward others in their weaknesses. Whatever the grace, the integrity involved in expressing ourselves so truly is its own grace.

> Many centuries of experience indicate that, in practice, the key to the humility of Christ is *openness of spirit* . . . We should take the initiative and make ourselves, our thoughts, desires and experiences, known to a spiritual guide, the novice director or the superior. Such openness—summed up somewhat imperfectly in Saint Benedict's fifth degree of humility—usually takes a certain time and is seldom without some stress or strain, but its fruit is the joy of being known and loved as you are. Real sincerity in love or growth in prayer is very seldom achieved without it, at least in our monasteries.[6]

Those who have experienced this even a little can pray with the psalmist:

> Many are the torments of the wicked;
> but steadfast love surrounds those who trust in the Lord.
> Be glad in the Lord and rejoice, O righteous,
> and shout for joy, all you upright in heart!

[5] Adrienne Von Speyr, *Confession* (San Francisco: Ignatius Press, 1985) 152.
[6] Augustine Roberts, *Centered on Christ* (Petersham: St. Bede's Publications, 1993) 154–155.

THE PENITENTIAL PSALMS

For I am ready to fall,
and my pain is ever with me.
I confess my iniquity;
I am sorry for my sin.
                    Psalm 38:17-18

"Against you, you alone, have I sinned."[1] Now we open onto a suite of rooms much loved and frequented over the centuries and traditionally called the penitential psalms: 6, 32, 38, 51, 102, 130, 143. They are most fitting companions for us as we travel daily the path of monastic conversion, balancing as they do three major themes:

1) The Experience of Sin

Sin may be experienced as forgetfulness or as turning in the wrong direction, as breaking a bond and as just plain heaviness. Death is its fruit.

2) The Experience of Sorrow

Sorrow for sin is a deeply purifying experience. In the Hebrew it sometimes has the sense of being crushed by one's sin and, in other cases, experiencing heaviness and fear over sin.

3) The Desire to Be Created Anew

The yearning within for forgiveness and atonement becomes a cry for total purity and newness:

"Create in me a clean heart, O God!"[2]

[1] Ps 51:4.
[2] Ps 51:10.

Let's focus here on sorrow. Saint Basil says that a psalm "creates a sorrow which is in accordance with God . . . and calls forth a tear even from a heart of stone."[3] From my own experience I can certainly say that these seven psalms, though not all equally, are one of God's greatest gifts in keeping us in touch with a true sorrow for sin and in giving us the words we need to pierce through the haziness of self-justification.

> For I am ready to fall,
> and my pain is ever with me.
> I confess my iniquity;
> I am sorry for my sin.[4]

"I am sorry." Very few words are as important in life. When one speaks these words genuinely they flow from the depths of the heart, and speaking them is the first and most essential, and sometimes only, remedy for the evil and sorrow we inflict on others. Indeed, it is often all another needs to hear to ease the pain and to bridge the gap. Because of its interior quality, its closeness to the human heart, to compassion and care and truth, sorrow for sin is the sacrificial offering that truly delights God:

> For you have no delight in sacrifice;
> If I were to give a burnt offering,
> you would not be pleased.
> The sacrifice acceptable to God is a broken spirit;
> a broken and contrite heart, O God, you will not despise.[5]

When we consider sin as breaking a bond with God, as infidelity in our relationship with him either directly or with another person made in his image and likeness; when we take this break to its ultimate conclusion of being separated from him forever in death, sorrow reaches a peak of intensity. Psalm 6 is expressive of this deep interior pain: "My soul is sorely troubled, agitated, terrified, amazed, ruined"[6]—these are the possibilities of meaning in the verb. These are words of agony, words which seem to have been stirring in Jesus' heart in his own agony:

---

[3] Saint Basil, *Homilies*, 153.
[4] Ps 38:17-18.
[5] Ps 51:16-17.
[6] Ps 6:3.

"My soul is very sorrowful, even to death";[7] "Now my soul is troubled. And what should I say—'Father, save me from this hour?' No, it is for this reason that I have come to this hour."[8]

Written before the revelation of eternal life, the psalmist sorrows over death and, more precisely, over the separation he will experience from God. We who have received the good news of eternal life with and in Christ, can still experience this pain of separation when we sin grievously. Then it is our turn to enter into the sorrow of this psalm with our whole heart:

> For in death there is no remembrance of you;
> in Sheol who can give you praise?
> I am weary with my moaning;
> every night I flood my bed with tears;
> I drench my couch with my weeping.
> My eye wastes away because of grief.[9]

Every time I come near even the possibility of separation from God through sin, I know without doubt that there is no sorrow like that sorrow, not poverty or affliction, humiliation or anything else. It is sharp and clean and deep; it awakens and quickens—and it is urgent. The dearest thing in life is at stake.

We get a sense of this in Psalm 32, for it describes the effects of sin in terms of the deepest possible heaviness and sluggishness. Actually this feeling is a great blessing, God's hand pressing upon us, as it were, until we can no longer bear it. Saying "I'm sorry" opens us to the first thrust of the surgeon's knife:

> While I kept silence, my body wasted away
> through my groaning all the day long.
> For night and day your hand was heavy upon me;
> my strength was dried up as by the heat of summer.
> Then I acknowledged my sin to you,
> and I did not hide my iniquity;
> I said, "I will confess my transgressions to the Lord,"
> and you forgave the guilt of my sin.[10]

[7] Mark 14:34.
[8] John 12:27-28.
[9] Ps 6:5-6.
[10] Ps 32:3-5.

You forgive. All sorrow moves toward this. From the depths of our being we stand on tiptoe, we peer through the night, we wait for the dawn of forgiving, renewing love:

> Out of the depths I cry to you, O Lord.
> Lord, hear my voice! . . .
> If you, O Lord, should mark iniquities,
> Lord, who could stand?
> But there is forgiveness with you . . .[11]

The word "forgive" in Psalm 32 has the sense of "bearing, supporting, taking away" and in Psalm 130 it is a "sending away" or a "letting go." Immediately there comes to mind that One who has borne our iniquities and taken away the sins of the world that we may let go of the past and enter into the joy of a new creation:

> Purge me with hyssop, and I shall be clean;
> wash me, and I shall be whiter than snow.
> Let me hear joy and gladness;
> let the bones that you have crushed rejoice.
> Hide your face from my sins,
> and blot out all my iniquities.
> Create in me a clean heart, O God,
> and put a new and right spirit within me.
> Do not cast me not away from your presence,
> and do not take your holy spirit from me.
> Restore to me the joy of your salvation.[12]

Sorrow for sin turned to joy has a special quality, something close to bittersweet, especially when we consider sin as forgetfulness. When we finally remember and turn to the Lord, we are often poignantly aware of how much he suffered for us and of how patiently and lovingly he has been waiting for us despite the ingratitude at the heart of forgetfulness. Our sorrow and our joy mingle to form the myrrh of which Bernard speaks: "Preserve without fail the memory of all those bitter things he endured for you, persevere in meditating on him . . . As for me,

[11] Ps 130:1, 3-4.
[12] Ps 51:7-12.

dear brothers, from the early years of my conversion, conscious
of my grave lack of merits, I made sure to gather for myself this
little bunch of myrrh and place it between my breasts. It was
culled from all the anxious hours and bitter experiences of my
Lord."[13]

Ultimately there is only one way in to the very depths of
the penitential psalms and that is through these anxious hours
and bitter experiences of our Lord, through the sorrow of Jesus
who knew well the truth of that universal prayer:

> Do not enter into judgment with your servant,
> for no one living is righteous before you.[14]

The Just One, the only Son, stood on trial for us and took the hard
road to Calvary, bearing our griefs all the way. John of Forde describes this beautifully in a passage worth quoting at length:

> We cannot mistake whose voice it is; it is the tender voice
> of Jesus speaking to sinners . . . Yes, it is Jesus who speaks
> to those who pass by the way, and asks them to see "if
> there is any sorrow like this." Yes, there are no tears like
> the tears of Jesus, no sorrow like the sorrow of Jesus. His
> sorrow breaks open the hardened heart of the sinner, and
> he repents. His tears draw a spring of tears from the rock
> of the desert. It is truly impossible for any soul not to be
> pierced sooner or later to contrition, and it was for this that
> Jesus shed tears. It is an established fact that Jesus grieved
> and wept, and over and above, offered his own self as a
> victim of reparation to his eternal Father for all those
> whom he foreknew and predestined to be restored
> through penance.
>
> So this is the loving lament of ancient compassion and
> eternal predestination:
>
> "I shall make you drunk with my tears, Heshbon and
> Elealeh." It is as if he lamented from the depths of his
> heart, speaking to the throng of sinners who would be jus-
> tified by the sacrament of penance. It is as if he says: I re-

---

[13] Bernard, *SC*, CF 7:221–222.
[14] Ps 143:2.

store on your account what you have stolen; I do penance
first for your sins. You, too, will be sorry, but it will be because of the tears of my penance rather than because of
your tears, that you will be justified. If you too are to feel
contrition, my tears will have to be your drink; if you are
to do real penance, my tears will have to make you drunk.
The pools of Heshbon, then, are the deep compassion of
God which made him do penance for sinners in the past
and the unfettered, secret inspiration of all repentance.[15]

Yes, his sorrow is truly that, the secret inspiration of all
repentance.

---

[15] John of Forde, *SC*, CF 45:165–166.

PSALM 45: LISTEN, O DAUGHTER

My heart overflows with a goodly theme;
I address my verses to the king;
my tongue is like the pen of a ready scribe.
You are the most handsome of men;
grace is poured upon your lips;
therefore God has blessed you forever.
Gird your sword on your thigh, O mighty one,
in your glory and majesty.
In your majesty ride on victoriously
for the cause of truth and to defend the right;
let your right hand teach you dread deeds.
Your arrows are sharp
in the heart of the king's enemies;
the peoples fall under you.
Your throne, O God, endures for ever and ever.
Your royal scepter is a scepter of equity;
you love righteousness and hate wickedness.
Therefore God, your God, has anointed you
with the oil of gladness beyond your companions;
your robes are all fragrant with myrrh and aloes and cassia.
From ivory palaces stringed instruments make you glad;
daughters of kings are among your ladies of honor;
at your right hand stands the queen in gold of Ophir.
Hear, O daughter, consider and incline your ear;
forget your people and your father's house,
and the king will desire your beauty.
Since he is your lord, bow to him;
the people of Tyre will seek your favor with gifts,
the richest of the people with all kinds of wealth.
The princess is decked in her chamber with gold-woven robes;

in many-colored robes she is led to the king;
behind her the virgins, her companions, follow.
With joy and gladness they are led along
as they enter the palace of the king.
In the place of ancestors you, O king, shall have sons;
you will make them princes in all the earth.
I will cause your name to be celebrated in all generations;
therefore the peoples will praise you forever and ever.

The great marriage hall! As we approach, the door is thrust open and we enter to festive sounds and joyous movements. The marriage of the Messiah has come and his bride has made herself ready.

If there is one psalm that hovers between the Psalms and the Song it is this one. Saint Bernard, following Origen, speaks of the psalms as the constant companions of our difficult and joyful experiences, but of the Song of Songs he says, "It stands at a point where all others culminate. Only the touch of the Spirit can inspire a song like this, and only personal experience can unfold its meaning. . . . For it is not a melody that resounds abroad but the very music of the heart, not a trilling on the lips but an inward pulsing of delight, a harmony not of voices but of wills. It is a tune you will not hear in the streets, these notes do not sound where crowds assemble; only the singer hears it and the one to whom he sings—the lover and the beloved."[1]

Psalm 45 celebrates this mystery of lover and beloved, singer and song, a mystery that will unfold fully in the Song. First it presents to us the Bridegroom, anointed with the oil of gladness and fairest among the sons of men. By his side stands the Queen Mother and approaching joyfully is the bride with her maiden companions. In the Song we will find all these personages again in one verse, the bride presupposed:

Look, O daughters of Zion,
at King Solomon,
at the crown with which his
mother crowned him

[1] Bernard, *SC*, CF 4:6-7.

> on the day of his wedding,
> on the day of the gladness of his heart.[2]

Let's look particularly at the bride and her companions. One has been singled out of many:

> Hear, O daughter, consider and
> incline your ear;
> forget your people and your father's house,
> and the king will desire your beauty.

This woman can say truly, "I am my beloved's and his desire is for me,"[3] she who once heard, "Your desire shall be for your husband."[4] And these maidens, her escort, so full of joy and gladness, so lacking in envy, what may we learn here about the one and the many, the chosen, and the companions of the chosen?

Saint Bernard delved into this mystery and expressed it with both profound and practical wisdom several times, for he knew well the meaning of the small white stone with the name known only to the one who receives it, the name that signifies our uniqueness before God. One Old Testament type of this uniqueness is Isaac who was an "only son" not in the sense of only begotten but of unlike any other,[5] a figure pointing to Jesus, the Only Son of the Father. Mystically and analogically we, too, have a share in this experience of feeling ourselves to be somehow incomparable, the "only one," perhaps particularly when we hear words like "Listen, O daughter, consider . . . forget your people and your father's house." And yet we know we share this blessed grace with others. How can this be?

Bernard speaks both experientially and theologically. First the experience:

> You would be very rash if you claimed to love him first or love him more; his love is greater, and it preceded yours. If the soul knows this—or because she knows it—is it any wonder that this soul, this bride, boasts that that great

[2] Song 3:11.
[3] Song 7:10.
[4] Gen 3:16.
[5] Gen 22:2, 12, 16.

majesty cares for her alone as though he had no others to care for, and she sets aside all her cares and devotes herself to him alone with all her heart. I must bring this sermon to an end, but I will say one thing to the spiritual among you, a strange thing, but true. The soul which looks on God sees him as though she alone were looked on by him. It is in this confidence that she says he is concerned for her, and she for him, and she sees nothing but herself and him. How good you are, Lord, to the soul who seeks you.[6]

And in another sermon:

I feel that the King has not one bedroom only, but several. For he has more than one queen . . . and each has her own secret rendezvous with the Bridegroom and says: "My secret to myself, my secret to myself." All do not experience the delight of the Bridegroom's private visit in the same room, the Father has different arrangements for each. For we did not choose him but he chose us and appointed places for us; and in the place of each one's appointment there he is too.[7]

When considering this experience theologically, Bernard turns to God's simplicity:

The essential simplicity of the Godhead is able to see many persons as if they were one, and one as if he were many, without division of attention between many or restriction to one, with no diminishment on the one hand or intensification on the other, being neither disturbed by anxieties nor troubled by cares; thus he may occupy himself with one without preoccupation, and with many without distraction.[8]

These considerations are so helpful in the formation process for as Dom Bernardo states, "It would appear that nuns" (and I would guess monks, too, to some degree) "in the novitiate and juniorate experience a bit of conflict in relation to their companions:

[6] Bernard, *SC*, CF 40:35.
[7] Bernard, *SC*, CF 7:33–34.
[8] Bernard, *SC*, CF 40:27–28.

a mixture of adhesion and rejection alternately or simultane-
ously. Most likely this is due to the need for identification and
differentiation with peers. When jealousy and envy are prop-
erly worked out and transformed into love, this can be the basis
of deep and lasting friendships."[9]

Differentiation: each of us is the bride and must develop
this sense ever more deeply through prayer; identification: each
of us is the bride's companion and must develop this sense ever
more deeply through mutual care and esteem. Here, too,
Bernard gives a way, that of ordered love: "Would that the Lord
Jesus would set in order in me the little fund of love he gave
me, that while my interest may extend to all his concerns, I may
be careful before everything else for the project or duty he has
appointed especially for me. . . . If I reveal genuine concern
for that which is my special charge and nevertheless a still finer
sympathy for a work that is greater, I find that I have fulfilled
the order of love in both ways."[10]

The King desires our beauty, and there are no two beauties
alike. We cannot imitate another but only seek to discover and
express the original in ourselves. Then together, in many-colored
robes, we may enter joyfully the palace of the King.

---

[9] Bernardo Olivera, "Our Young—And Not So Young—Monks and Nuns,"
Conference given at the General Chapter, September 2002, 12.
[10] Bernard, *SC*, CF 41:26-27.

PSALM 46: EMMANUEL, GOD WITH US

God is our refuge and strength,
a very present help in trouble.
Therefore we will not fear, though the earth should change,
though the mountains shake in the heart of the sea;
though its waters roar and foam,
though the mountains tremble with its tumult.
There is a river whose streams make glad the city of God,
the holy habitation of the Most High.
God is in the midst of the city;
it shall not be moved;
God will help it when morning dawns.
The nations are in an uproar, the kingdoms totter;
he utters his voice, the earth melts.
The Lord of hosts is with us;
the God of Jacob is our refuge.
Come, behold the works of the Lord;
see what desolations he has brought on the earth.
He makes wars cease to the end of the earth;
he breaks the bow, and shatters the spear;
he burns the shields with fire.
"Be still, and know that I am God!
I am exalted among the nations,
I am exalted in the earth."
The Lord of hosts is with us;
the God of Jacob is our refuge.

"The Lord of hosts is with us; the God of Jacob is our refuge." Like waves of gladness this refrain of Psalm 46 rises in our hearts as we enter the room of Emmanuel. With us. The preposition is powerful. It is essential. It is not to be toned down

73

for the sake of the relatively more significant words, but shouted for all we are worth. "With," together forever in life and in death!

"With us" is our response to God's word, "I am with you," a word of mission and a promise of support. Recall Jacob: "Behold I am with you and will keep you wherever you go";[1] Gideon: "The Lord is with you, you mighty man of valor";[2] then the entire people Israel: "Fear not, for I am with you, be not dismayed, for I am your God; I will strengthen you, I will help you, I will uphold you by my victorious right hand."[3] And finally recall the handmaid of the Lord who carries in her heart all the hopes and dreams of Israel: "Do not be afraid, Mary, the Lord is with you."[4] Of her is born the conviction, incarnate, that God is with us, Emmanuel.

Although it is generally not easy to pin down historical references in the psalms, this song of Zion surely has the flavor of Isaiah, the prophet of Emmanuel, in his insistence that Judah remain interiorly still in a total trust that God was with Jerusalem and would not permit her to be invaded by Assyria. And so it happened. One day Sennacherib was outside the gates; the next day he was gone:[5]

> There is a river whose streams make glad the city of God,
> the holy habitation of the Most High.
> God is in the midst of the city, it shall not be moved;
> God will help it when the morning dawns. . . .
> Come, behold the works of the Lord,
> see what desolations he has brought on the earth.
> He makes wars cease to the end of the earth;
> he breaks the bow, and shatters the spear;
> he burns the shields with fire!
> Be still, and know that I am God!

This unutterable stillness in wondrous knowing comes when the might and mercy of God vindicate our trust, often in struggles that are all the more painful because hidden. It comes,

[1] Gen 28:15.
[2] Judg 6:13.
[3] Isa 41:10.
[4] Luke 1:29.
[5] See Isa 37.

too, in the mystery of Christmas, the feast of Emmanuel. For me the graced moment is always the late afternoon of Christmas Eve, an hour or so before Vespers, when suddenly I know that the two mystic riders have arrived again in our land. As they make their way to Bethlehem sharing an immense joy and a sacred trust, I drop everything to follow them: my wars, my bows, my spears, my fears, and I am still before my God. Mary and Joseph hold the secret: He is with us, we are with him. All of life moves toward the fulfillment of this mystery of being-with.

> You have died and your life is hid *with Christ* in God.[6]

> My desire is to depart and be *with Christ*.[7]

> Then we who are alive, who are left, shall be caught up together with them in the clouds to meet the Lord in the air: and *so we shall always be with the Lord*.[8]

We contemplatives for whom the "cloister responds to the need, felt as paramount, to be with the Lord,"[9] can offer this word we live to a hungry world, hungry to know in its very depths that the Lord of hosts is with us, with us always, even until the end of time.

---

[6] Col 3:3.
[7] Phil 1:23.
[8] 1 Thess 4:17.
[9] *Vita Consecrata*, number 59.

PSALM 51: THE HEART

Have mercy on me, O God,
according to your steadfast love;
according to your abundant mercy
blot out my transgressions.
Wash me thoroughly from my iniquity,
and cleanse me from my sin.
For I know my transgressions,
and my sin is ever before me.
Against you, you alone, have I sinned,
and done what is evil in your sight,
so that you are justified in your sentence
and blameless when you pass judgement.
Indeed, I was born guilty,
a sinner when my mother conceived me.
You desire truth in the inward being;
therefore teach me wisdom in my secret heart.
Purge me with hyssop, and I shall be clean;
wash me, and I shall be whiter than snow.
Let me hear joy and gladness;
let the bones that you have crushed rejoice.
Hide your face from my sins,
and blot out all my iniquities.
Create in me a clean heart, O God,
and put a new and right spirit within me.
Do not cast me away from your presence,
and do not take your holy spirit from me.
Restore to me the joy of your salvation,
and sustain in me a willing spirit.
Then I will teach transgressors your ways,
and sinners will return to you.

Deliver me from bloodshed, O God,
O God of my salvation,
and my tongue will sing aloud of your deliverance.
O Lord, open my lips,
and my mouth will declare your praise.
For you have no delight in sacrifice;
if I were to give a burnt offering, you would not be pleased.
The sacrifice acceptable to God is a broken spirit;
a broken and contrite heart,
O God, you will not despise.
Do good to Zion in your good pleasure;
rebuild the walls of Jerusalem,
then you will delight in right sacrifices,
in burnt offerings and whole burnt offerings;
then bulls will be offered on your altar.

Psalm 51 is a room at the top, a room to which the people of God took many years of stairs to climb. When we enter we kneel before the secret revealed there, the simple truth that God desires nothing so much as the human heart, broken, pure, and wise. From its windows we catch a glimpse, far off on the horizon, of someone approaching, that One who penetrated in a unique and unrepeatable way into the mystery of our humanity, into our heart, in order to reveal us to ourselves.[1] Behold he comes, the Merciful Heart, in whose image we were made:

Have mercy on me, O God, according to your steadfast love; according to your abundant mercy blot our my transgressions.

THE BROKEN HEART

The sacrifice acceptable to God is a broken spirit; a broken and contrite heart, O God, you will not despise.

Although I have already spoken of sorrow for sin in relation to the penitential psalms, I would like to say a bit more about its relation to the heart of Christ. Sorrow flows most

[1] See John Paul II, First Encyclical Letter, *The Redeemer of Man* (Rome, 1979) number 8.

freely when we recognize the one whom we have pierced by our depravity, mourning for him as for an only Son:

> Against you, you alone have I sinned.

The sight of his wounded heart pierces our hardness as nothing else, for when the "secret of his heart is laid open through the clefts of his body, that mighty mystery of loving,"[2] then we experience what Saint Bernard described:

> Easily they love more who realize they are loved more . . .
> The Church sees King Solomon with the diadem his mother had placed on his head. She sees the Father's only Son carrying his cross, the Lord of majesty, slapped and covered with spittle; she sees the Author of life and glory pierced by nails, wounded by a lance, saturated with abuse, and finally laying down his precious life for his friends. As she beholds this, the sword of love transfixes all the more her soul.[3]

The recognition of his great love for us is the sword that breaks the heart so that floods of longing may pour forth in the cry, "Create in me a pure heart, O God!" This cry is echoed powerfully in the words of our Father, Baldwin of Forde, when he prays, "Take from me, O Lord, my heart of stone. Take away my hardened heart. Take away my uncircumcised heart. Give me a new heart, a heart of flesh, a pure heart! You who purify the heart, you who love the pure heart, possess my heart and dwell within it, enclosing it and filling it, higher than what in me is highest, more inward than my most inward part. O form of beauty and seal of sanctity, seal my heart in your image, seal my heart under your mercy, O God of my heart, O God my portion for ever."[4]

---

[2] Bernard, *SC*, CF 31:144.

[3] Bernard, *Liber de diligendo Deo, Tractates II*. Cistercian Fathers series 13 (Washington, D.C.: Cistercian Publications, 1974) 99.

[4] Baldwin, *Tractates*, CF 41:83.

THE PURE HEART

Create in me a pure heart, O God!

The pure heart is born of God's mercy that washes our broken hearts more and more and that shines on them like the sun. In Saint Gertrud's words, "The gaze of the divine loving-kindness, like the sun, rendered the soul dazzling white and purified from all stains, whiter than snow. That effect is acquired through humble acknowledgment of one's own faults."[5]

Saint Bernard, too, will speak of merciful love as the path to purity of heart, but from another angle, that of our own mercy toward others. For when we come to know our personal sinfulness and weakness we are much more disposed to compassionate others: "You will never have real mercy for the failings of another until you know and realize that you have the same failings in your soul."[6] This sympathy, in turn, leads to clear-sightedness, to the pure heart which sees truth:

> If they now ignore Truth, needy, naked and unimpressive, all too late they will blush to see Truth come in might and power . . . Then indeed they will know the Lord when he comes to do judgment, though now they choose to ignore him when he pleads for mercy. Then they will look on him whom they have pierced and whom they have spurned in their greed. Now is the time to clear the eyes of the heart of every speck of weakness, ignorance and jealousy by weeping, zeal for justice and perseverance in works of mercy and then to those purified eyes the promise of Truth will be fulfilled: "Blessed are the clean of heart for they shall see God."[7]

The pure heart, then, is not only free from vice but full of love. As Saint Benedict reminds us, this is what God hears when we come to prayer, the pure heart, the broken heart, and nothing else.[8]

---

[5] Gertrud, *SC,* CF 63:132.
[6] Bernard, *Hum,* CF 13:35.
[7] Bernard, *Hum,* CF 13:47.
[8] See RB 20:3.

THE WISE HEART

> You desire truth in the inward being;
> therefore teach me wisdom in my secret heart.

The Psalmist longs for a heart completely true and wise and, indeed, this gift awaits him through union with the one in whom all the treasures of wisdom and knowledge abide. The Heart draws near:

> The nail cries out, the wound cries out that God is truly in Christ, reconciling the world to himself. "The iron pierced his soul" and his heart has drawn near, so that he is no longer one who cannot sympathize with my weaknesses.[9]

The Heart speaks, "What do you wish?" Let Lutgard answer for all of us, "I want your Heart." The Heart responds, "Nay, rather it is I Who want your heart."[10]

Encouraged by his desire, we draw near, longing to be one with him. Our Fathers loved to describe this union in Paul's phrase, "one spirit with him,"[11] whereas our Mothers tended toward the Johannine imagery of the heart, speaking in terms of "one heart" or even an exchange of hearts. The reality is that in this union we discover, at last, Truth in the heart and Wisdom in the inmost being, and in this discovery we know the power of John's words: "Out of his heart shall flow rivers of living water."[12] Our heart in his, his heart in ours, this is the source of all apostolic fruitfulness.

> She (Gertrud) offered the Lord her own heart in these terms: "Here is my heart, Lord. . . ." The Son of God appeared, offering God the Father her heart united with his own divine Heart in the likeness of a chalice, its two parts joined together with wax. When she saw this she said to the Lord with suppliant devotion, "Most loving God,

---

[9] Bernard, *SC*, CF 31:143-144.

[10] *Lives of Ida of Nivelles, Lutgard and Alice the Leper* (Lafayette, Oregon: Guadalupe Translations, 1987) 13.

[11] 1 Cor 6:17.

[12] John 7:38.

grant that my heart may be always at hand, like the flasks which are brought for the lords' refreshment, so that you may always, as you please, have it clean for pouring in and pouring out whenever you wish, for whomever you please." The Son of God kindly accepted this and said to the Father, "Holy Father, may this heart pour out, to your eternal praise, all that my Heart contained for dispensation in my human nature."[13]

The heart of Christ in us, broken, pure, and wise, is truly the heart of Psalm 51."What has been said so often and so inadequately is true: The heart of Jesus Christ is the beginning and end of all things."[14]

[13] Gertrud, *Herald*, CF 63:103–104.
[14] Romano Guardini, *The Lord* (Chicago: Henry Regnery Company, 1954) 400.

PSALM 55:
SOLITUDE AND COMMUNITY

Give ear to my prayer, O God;
do not hide yourself from my supplication.
Attend to me, and answer me;
I am troubled in my complaint.
I am distraught by the noise of the enemy,
because of the clamor of the wicked.
For they bring trouble upon me,
and in anger they cherish enmity against me.
My heart is in anguish within me,
the terrors of death have fallen upon me.
Fear and trembling come upon me,
and horror overwhelms me.
And I say, "O that I had wings like a dove!
I would fly away and be at rest;
truly, I would flee far away;
I would hurry to find a shelter for myself
from the raging wind and tempest."
Confuse, O Lord, confound their speech;
for I see violence and strife in the city.
Day and night they go around it on its walls,
and iniquity and trouble are within it;
ruin is in its midst;
oppression and fraud
do not depart from its market place.
It is not enemies who taunt me—
I could bear that;
it is not adversaries who deal insolently with me—
I could hide from them.
But it is you, my equal,

my companion, my familiar friend,
with whom I kept pleasant company;
we walked in the house of God with the throng.
Let death come upon them;
let them go down alive to Sheol;
for evil is in their homes and in their hearts.
But I call upon God,
and the Lord will save me.
Evening and morning and at noon
I utter my complaint and moan,
and he will hear my voice.
He will redeem me unharmed
from the battle that I wage,
for many are arrayed against me.
God, who is enthroned from of old,
will hear, and will humble them—
because they do not change,
and do not fear God.
My companion laid hands on a friend
and violated a covenant with me
with speech smoother than butter,
but with a heart set on war;
with words that were softer than oil,
but in fact were drawn swords.
Cast your burden on the Lord,
and he will sustain you;
he will never permit
the righteous to be moved.
But you, O God, will cast them down
into the lowest pit;
the bloodthirsty and treacherous
shall not live out half their days.
But I will trust in you.

Some of the rooms of the Psalter-mansion open onto gardens, and here, unmistakably, onto the garden of Gethsemani. Saint John tells us that after the Last Supper Jesus crossed the Kidron valley and entered a garden, a garden found all the more easily by Judas who, with the other disciples had met there often with Jesus.[1] A place of friendship and communion, a beloved place, it was ill-suited for betrayal. In Psalm 55 we catch a glimpse of this loving communion: ". . . it is you, my equal, my companion, my familiar friend, with whom I kept pleasant company; we walked in the house of God with the throng." And yet the betrayal!

> It is not enemies who taunt me—
> I could bear that;
> it is not adversaries who deal insolently with me—
> I could hide from them.
> But it is you . . . my friend.

In the face of this betrayal the heart flees into solitude: "O that I had wings like a dove! I would fly away and be at rest; truly, I would flee far away; I would lodge in the wilderness; I would hurry to find a shelter for myself from the raging wind and tempest."

Solitude comes about in many ways, some of them as unexpected as betrayal, but no matter what its source, a mysterious blend of solitude and communion is at the heart of every life and, in particular, of our life, for one of the clearest signs of the Cistercian call is an instinctive openness "to both the solitary and communal dimensions of the life."[2] When in harmony Cistercian solitude and community look like this:

> By the wonderful favor of God's loving care, in this solitude of ours we have the peace of solitude and yet we do not lack the consolation and comfort of holy companionship. It is possible for each of us to sit alone and be silent, because we have no one to disturb us with interruptions, and yet it cannot be said of us: "Woe to him who is alone, since he has nobody to console him or if he should fall has none to lift him up." We are surrounded by companions, yet we are not in a crowd. We live as it were in a city, yet we have to contend with no tumult, so the voice of one crying in the wilderness can be heard by us, provided only

[1] See John 18:1-2.
[2] *Ratio Institutionis, Guidelines on Formation,* OCSO, number 22.

that we have interior silence to correspond to the exterior silence that surrounds us.[3]

Although this grace of the desert as described by Guerric is truly our Cistercian grace, we all have a fair share of less harmonious moments, and Psalm 55 is a garden to which we may safely flee when our lack of integration of community and solitude becomes an agony, a garden where we may cast our cares upon the Lord who cares for us. We may not live with false brethren, but surely we must learn to live with what is false in our brothers and sisters, and most of all with what is false in ourselves, trusting in the grace of continual conversion. We must learn to enter the solitude of limitations, the limitations of sinfulness as well as the limitations of circumstances and gifts, and find in these limits the very shape of our call. It is often the unwanted and unexpected solitudes that stretch us beyond ourselves and make us roomy for God, make of us a heaven for God.

How many of us were able for the first time to name this mysterious yearning for solitude within us when we came across these words of Thomas Merton:

> I will give you what you desire. I will lead you into solitude. I will lead you by the way you cannot possibly understand because I want it to be the quickest way. Therefore all the things around you will be armed against you, to deny you, to hurt you, to give you pain, and therefore to reduce you to solitude. Because of their enmity, you will soon be left alone. They will cast you out and forsake you and reject you and you will be alone. Everything that touches you will burn you, and you will draw your hand away in pain, until you have withdrawn yourself from all things. Then you will be alone. Everything that can be desired will sear you, and brand you with a cautery, and you will fly from it in pain, to be alone. Every created joy will only come to you as pain, and you will die to all joy and be left alone . . . In that day you shall begin to possess the solitude you have so long desired. And your solitude will bear immense fruit in the souls of men you will never see

---

[3] Guerric, *Sermo in adventu domini*, CF 8:23–24.

on earth. Do not ask when it will be or where it will be or
how it will be: On a mountain or in a prison, in a desert or
in a concentration camp or in a hospital or at Gethsemani.
It does not matter. So do not ask me, because I am not
going to tell you. You will not know until you are in it.[4]

But when we are in it we know. "Evening, morn and noon"
we recognize our personal Gethsemani where we are privileged to "taste the true solitude of Jesus' anguish and poverty."[5]
With him we learn to pray Psalm 55 from the inside, embracing
the tension between community and solitude without bitterness or alienation, humbly realizing that each person's unique
and unrepeatable journey to God will bring him or her to solitudes that no one has entered before in quite the same way. At
those moments, exposed to our utter resourcelessness, we learn
to rely absolutely on the Father and to pray to him with Jesus,
"For my part, I put my trust in you."

---

[3] Thomas Merton, *The Seven Storey Mountain* (New York: Harcourt, Brace and
Company, 1948) 422.
[4] See Merton, *Seven Storey Mountain*, 422.

PSALM 58: A GOOD CURSE

Do you indeed decree what is right, you gods?
Do you judge people fairly?
No, in your hearts you devise wrongs;
your hands deal out violence on earth.
The wicked go astray from the womb;
they err from their birth, speaking lies.
They have venom like the venom of a serpent,
like the deaf adder that stops its ear,
so that it does not hear the voice of charmers
or of the cunning enchanter.
O God, break the teeth in their mouths;
tear out the fangs of the young lions, O Lord!
Let them vanish like water that runs away;
like grass let them be trodden down and wither.
Let them be like the snail that dissolves into slime;
like the untimely birth that never sees the sun.
Sooner than your pots can feel the heat of thorns,
whether green or ablaze, may he sweep them away!
The righteous will rejoice when they see vengeance done;
they will bathe their feet in the blood of the wicked.
People will say, "Surely there is a reward for the righteous;
surely there is a God who judges on earth."

Do you dare not knock at the door of this psalm? Do the curses within repel and frighten you? Don't pass by so hurriedly for here, yes, here too, there is a treasure. How could it be otherwise since our Lord Jesus entered in before us and made even cursing new.

First we hear a cry of just anger against those who deal out violence on the earth, an energy we should rightly feel against evil, both the evil in others and in ourselves. Then we have an incomparable description of the wicked in the likeness of a snake:

> The wicked go astray from the womb;
> they err from their birth, speaking lies,
> They have venom like the venom of a serpent,
> like the deaf adder that stops its ear
> so that it does not hear the voice of charmers
> or of the cunning enchanter.

When we protect ourselves from such imagery, what we miss! If a community chooses for certain reasons to exclude such phrases from the Divine Office, let us at least expose ourselves to them privately, for do they not provide for us the perfect mirror of our more perverse movements and our stubborn roots? How the Divine Charmer calls and how we resist his voice. Have you ever overheard one of the thoughts in you, be it gluttony, lust, anger, etc., having a whispered conversation in one of the corners of the house and, instead of confronting it and choosing against its ruinous course, put on spiritual ear plugs? When we use such psalms as mirrors we have a better chance of not deceiving ourselves. In the words of Saint Athanasius: "And among all the books, the Psalter has certainly a very special grace, a choiceness of quality well worthy to be pondered; for, besides the characteristics which it shares with others, it has this peculiar marvel of its own, that within it are represented and portrayed in all their variety the movements of the human soul. It is like a picture in which you see yourself portrayed, and, seeing, may understand and consequently form yourself upon the pattern given."[1]

This look at ourselves gives us a certain objective distance from our snakelike ways and more space to choose wisely. Blessed be the times that we listen to the Enchanter and cry out, not against flesh and blood, but against the principalities and powers:

> Let them vanish like water that runs away;
> like grass let them be trodden down and wither.

---

[1] Saint Athanasius, *Epistola ad Marcellinum*, 103.

Let them be like the snail that dissolves into slime;
like the untimely birth that never sees the sun.

What a perfect end for evil! What a good outlet for a curse!

PSALM 63: DESIRE IN THE NIGHT

O God, you are my God, for you I long;
for you my soul is thirsting.
My body pines for you
like a dry, weary land without water.
So I gaze on you in the sanctuary
to see your strength and your glory.
For your love is better than life,
my lips will speak your praise.
So I will bless you all my life,
in your name I will lift up my hands.
My soul shall be filled as with a banquet,
my mouth shall praise you with joy.
On my bed I remember you.
On you I muse through the night
for you have been my help;
in the shadow of your wings I rejoice.
My soul clings to you;
your right hand holds me fast.
Those who seek to destroy my life
shall go down to the depths of the earth.
They shall be put into the power of the sword
and left as the prey of the jackals.
But the king shall rejoice in God;
(all that swear by him shall be blessed)
for the mouth of liars shall be silenced.[1]

Busy, preoccupied, on the verge of lateness, I walked quickly to my place one late afternoon in May for the first Ves-

[1] The Grail Psalter.

pers of Ascension. Soft light filled our church. I would have liked to kneel in that light and prepare my heart for the prayer of Christ, but the solemn bells, the organ, the sign of the Cross, the hymn—all rose rapidly like a river of praise, carrying my body but not my mind. And then, stillness. A voice intoned the first psalm of the feast:

O God, you are my God, for you I long.

It was the voice of Jesus, the single voice that contains all voices, the voice of the only Son. At that moment I understood the meaning of desire. Desire is to be inside the yearning of Jesus Christ for his Father.

This moment illumined a pathway for me into the psalms, the path of Jesus' experience. The beautiful words of Augustine on Psalm 85 come to mind: "Let us then recognize both our voice in his, and his voice in ours. . . . In other parts of Scripture we hear him as one sighing, praying, giving praise and thanks. . . . Our minds find nothing in Scripture that does not go back to him, nothing that will allow us to stray from him."[2]

This yearning of Jesus on the eve of his Ascension, was it not also his yearning during his long nights of prayer? We who are so devoted to the night, who begin each day long before dawn, are we not devoted to his desire in the night? When we enter Psalm 63 by way of Jesus, we enter by way of the Image in which we were created. We touch the hunger and thirst that were imprinted on the human soul from the beginning of time, making us *capax Dei*, vast interior space, dry weary land without water.

Desire is related to emptiness, not fullness, and it takes different shapes: acute longing as in thirst; a more sustainable ache as in hunger; inexplicable groanings, often barely audible, which form the ineradicable ground of our being. Desire takes such a strong hold of the monastic heart that it moves us to watch in the night, every night, with Jesus and for Jesus. Sometimes we are not exactly sure why we should remain in that empty darkness after the psalms of the Night Office, but one

[2] Saint Augustine, *In Ps 85, A Word in Season: Lent–Easter Triduum* (Villanova: Augustinian Press, 1987) 165–166.

thing we do know: we cannot go away. Our desire is not of our own making. It was conceived in an immense Desire which long preceded and pursued us: "Do you keep watch? He keeps watch also. If you rise at night before the time of vigil and hasten to anticipate the morning watch, you will find him there. He will always be waiting for you."[3]

[3] Bernard, *SC*, CF 40:35.

PSALM 73:
THE SIXTH STEP OF HUMILITY

Truly God is good to the upright,
to those who are pure in heart.
But as for me, my feet had almost stumbled;
my steps had nearly slipped.
For I was envious of the arrogant;
I saw the prosperity of the wicked.
For they have no pain;
their bodies are sound and sleek.
They are not in trouble as others are;
they are not plagued like other people.
Therefore pride is their necklace;
violence covers them like a garment.
Their eyes swell out with fatness;
their hearts overflow with follies.
They scoff and speak with malice;
loftily they threaten oppression.
They set their mouths against heaven,
and their tongues range over the earth.
Therefore the people turn and praise them,
and find no fault in them.
And they say, "How can God know?
Is there knowledge in the Most High?"
Such are the wicked;
always at ease, they increase in riches.
All in vain I have kept my heart clean
and washed my hands in innocence.
For all day long I have been plagued,
and am punished every morning.

If I had said, "I will talk on in this way,"
I would have been untrue to the circle of your children.
But when I thought how to understand this,
it seemed to me a wearisome task,
until I went into the sanctuary of God;
then I perceived their end.
Truly you set them in slippery places;
you make them fall to ruin.
How they are destroyed in a moment,
swept away utterly by terrors!
They are like a dream when one awakes;
on awaking you despise them like phantoms.
When my soul was embittered,
when I was pricked in heart,
I was stupid and ignorant;
I was like a brute beast toward you.
Nevertheless I am continually with you;
you hold my right hand.
You guide me with your counsel,
and afterward you will receive me with honor.
Whom have I in heaven but you?
And there is nothing on earth that I desire other than you.
My flesh and my heart may fail,
but God is the strength of my heart and my portion forever.
Indeed, those who are far from you will perish;
you put an end to those who are false to you.
But for me it is good to be near God;
I have made the Lord God my refuge,
to tell of all your works.

For me the sixth step of humility, joy in the lowest, best discloses its meaning in light of Psalm 73 with all its mystical depths of intimacy, beauty, and pain. In fact, in a very real sense Psalm 73, the only biblical reference Benedict uses here, is itself the sixth step of humility. Let's look at it carefully.

The movement of this psalm is from temptation to contentment. A poor and faithful man is severely tempted to envy, and in the process of resisting this vice he is transformed into a poor man filled with joy and unutterable riches. What is at work here is the mystery of *tentatio* and the victory of *contemplatio*.

Within the movement of *lectio, meditatio, oratio, contemplatio,* Martin Luther inserted tentatio, that is, struggle with a word of God that challenges us.[1] The psalmist expresses this struggle and temptation in vivid images. He observes the luxury of the wicked and wonders how it can be that God seemingly blesses them while abandoning the faithful one, at least this faithful one, to his affliction. Is God's retribution unjust?

> Every morning is punishment to me;
> every day I am beaten.
> Why did I ever have faith in you?[2]

Yet despite all this, the psalmist clings to his faith, his heart dying and humbled and pierced, as he cries out, "How could I deny the faith of my fathers?" He feels like a beast before God. His lot is the poorest and the worst of everything. Then comes the moment of light. Within his poverty and not apart from it, he experiences profound communion with God and passes to another level of consciousness wherein he knows that God's presence is stronger than death and more desirable than riches. In fact, it contains all riches. This is the secret of the sixth step of humility. One has passed from enduring the poorest and the worst to delighting in them because one has discovered the pearl beyond price. As Delatte states: "We are not poor in order to be poor, but to be rich with God and rich like God."[3]

Cistercians have always been drawn to this poverty that is rich with God; "to be poor with the poor Christ"[4] as our fathers put it. What are our opportunities for practicing the poorest and the worst? Seemingly little things, yet they cost us everything: not manipulating to change one's circumstances; accepting it

---

[1] Ghislain Lafont, from a talk to the U.S. Novice Directors at Gethsemani Abbey, June 1990.

[2] The translation of Psalm 73 used within the text is from *Fifty Psalms,* Huub Oosterhuis and others (New York: The Seabury Press, 1968) 73–74.

[3] Paul Delatte, *The Rule of Saint Benedict: A Commentary* (London: Burns Oates and Washbourne Limited, 1921) 345.

[4] *Exordium* 15:33, Waddell, 435.

when one is overlooked; not comparing one's lot with that of others; not giving in to curiosity and envy; being content with what is sufficient and simple in food, clothing, and other necessities; putting one's heart into the work one is given. It is particularly this last point that can stretch us, for our work is, for the most part, manual, simple, hard, and very short on prestige. In fact there's just so little of the latter to go around that one has to come to terms with the fact quickly and enter either into jealous competition or into the cathartic experience of the psalmist. In the sanctuary of our souls we are pierced with the deeper meaning of such a humble existence. It lies, once again, in the words, "*With* you."

"With you." Those words are the secret joy in both Psalm 73 and in the sixth step of humility:

> I was embittered and rebellious,
> I was hurt
> deep in my soul.
> I was like a senseless
> animal with you.
> With you, I am
> always with you.
> You hold me tight,
> Your hand in mine.
> You will bring all things
> to a good end,
> You lead me on in your good pleasure.
> What is heaven to me without you,
> Where am I on earth
> if you are not there?

And from the Rule: "The sixth step of humility is that a monk should be content with the most common and worst of everything, and in all that is required of him to judge himself a bad and worthless worker, saying of himself with the prophet: I was reduced to nothing and did not realize it; I have become like a beast before you, yet I am always with you."[5]

---

[5] RB 7:49-50.

"With you" implies communion, intimacy. It is the intimate presence of a person, the Person of Jesus, in the monk's life. In a homily for monastic profession Karl Rahner states that for many Christians this presence "can be combined with the thousand and more possibilities of an earthly rich and totally developed human existence," but for the monk it is most compatible with poverty. As he describes it, "It also can be that . . . a Christian may arrive at the frightening stage where he is willing to base his whole life on this distant God, to rush toward this distant horizon of life, as if there would be nothing worth stopping for between him and this infinite distance."[6]

Our whole *conversatio* disposes us to this. Our labor in particular, marked though it is by all the essentials of truly human and Christian labor—creativity, solidarity, redemptive love, responsibility, struggle—offers us primarily the possibility of having no "reason to exist apart from the Beloved."[7] Its relative unimportance is our very way into his presence, since through it we can often combine Mary's rest at the feet of Jesus with Martha's generous service. One does not arrive at this abiding disposition without the long struggle of which the psalmist is such a model, but when one does it becomes impossible to remain focused on lesser desires. One has acquired a taste for the divine and can find joy only with God. What the psalmist concludes, "To be near God is my happiness!" William of St. Thierry, speaking for monks, echoes centuries later: "It is for others to serve God, it is for you to cling to him; it is for others to believe in God, know him, love him and revere him; it is for you to taste him, understand him, be acquainted with him, enjoy him."[8]

---

[6] Karl Rahner, *Meditations on the Sacraments* (New York: The Seabury Press, 1977) 97.

[7] Roberts, *Centered on Christ*, 34.

[8] William, *Ep frat*, CF 12:14.

PSALM 91: OVERSHADOWING

You who live in the shelter of the Most High,
who abide in the shadow of the Almighty,
will say to the Lord, "My refuge and my fortress;
my God, in whom I trust."
For he will deliver you from the snare of the fowler
and from the deadly pestilence;
he will cover you with his pinions,
and under his wings you will find refuge;
his faithfulness is a shield and buckler.
You will not fear the terror of the night,
or the arrow that flies by day,
or the pestilence that stalks in darkness,
or the destruction that wastes at noonday.
A thousand may fall at your side,
ten thousand at your right hand,
but it will not come near you.
You will only look with your eyes
and see the punishment of the wicked.
Because you have made the Lord your refuge,
the Most High your dwelling place,
no evil shall befall you,
no scourge come near your tent.
For he will command his angels concerning you
to guard you in all your ways.
On their hands they will bear you up,
so that you will not dash your foot against a stone.
You will tread on the lion and the adder,
the young lion and the serpent you will trample under foot.
Those who love me, I will deliver;

I will protect those who know my name.
When they call to me, I will answer them;
I will be with them in trouble,
I will rescue them and honor them.
With long life I will satisfy them,
and show them my salvation.

Day is done. She who has borne its labors and trials finds rest in the sanctuary:

> You who live in the shelter (literally, "secret place") of the
>   Most High,
> who abide in the shadow of the Almighty,
> will say to the Lord, "My refuge and my fortress; my God, in
>   whom I trust."

Terror has no strength against this shelter where we are encircled by love. We experience this intimately as the shadows fall upon the day and, wrapped in night, we sing the song of the great Encircling One. Who is he who lets us abide under his wings? What shade can compare with that he offers—so dark, our enemies cannot find us; so bright we cannot fail to find him? How he loves to encircle us, this Great Eagle, with the pinions of his deliverance; with his faithfulness; with his angels; with himself. Our part is to abide and be still, to cling and to trust.

That most ancient image of the eagle, symbol of God's tender and powerful care for his people, reminds us night after night, that he has carried us on his wings to himself this day and that he alone has led us through "a place of horror and of vast solitude"—our Fathers' description of Citeaux![1] Jesus will use a more diminutive image but not a less tender one: "O Jerusalem, Jerusalem . . . how often would I have gathered your children together as a hen gathers her brood under her wings."[2] His wings are for hiding; in God alone we are safely hidden from all that would hurt or destroy.

---

[1] *Exordium Cistercii* as in Chrysogonus Waddell, *Narrative and Legislative Texts from Early Citeaux* (Citeaux: Commentarii cistercienses, 1999) 400.
[2] Luke 13:34.

This hiddenness in God's secret place is an image of our monastic vocation, something Saint Bernard expressed so well in his commentary on Psalm 91:

> Beneath these shoulders we receive then four benefits: beneath them we are hidden; beneath them we are protected from the attacks of hawks and kites—the powers of the air; beneath this saving shadow we are refreshed and shaded from the excessive heat of the sun; beneath them, too, we are fed and nurtured. . . . It is necessary for us to lie hidden if we have a precious thing, for it is the treasure of the kingdom of heaven which a man found and hid away. This is why we hide bodily in cloisters and in forests. Do you wonder what we gain by this hiddenness? There is no one here, I believe, who were he to do in the world a quarter of what he does here, would not be revered as a saint, reckoned as an angel, whereas now he is daily rebuked and chided as negligent. Do you think it no small advantage not to be taken for a saint before actually being one? Would you not be afraid that, having already received this cheap reward, you would have no future reward? So it is necessary for all this to lie hidden not only from other people's eyes but from your own as well, and even more necessary . . . . This hiddenness, which we have already said is afforded beneath the Lord's shoulders, is something very similar to the overshadowing which came upon Mary from the Holy Spirit to conceal an incomprehensible mystery.[3]

This thought is sublime. The Cistercian life is a share in the overshadowing of Mary by the Holy Spirit. What she experienced in that moment—the deep into which he led her, the infusion in which he grounded her existence, the absolute trust and the surrender ordered to the conception of Christ-life—becomes our path too from our very first day in the monastery: "Formation to Cistercian life has for its purpose the restoration of the divine likeness in the sisters through the working of the Holy Spirit. Aided by the maternal care of the Mother of God, the sis-

---

[3] Saint Bernard, *Sermo super psalmum Qui habitat, Sermons on Conversion.* Cistercian Fathers series 25 (1981) 137–138.

ters so advance in the monastic way of life that they progressively attain the full measure of the stature of Christ."[4]

Mary is the one most able to help us recognize and welcome the Spirit wherever he breathes. As Guerric of Igny says so beautifully:

> If then God reckons as done to himself the kindness shown to his members, how much more will he recall with thanksgiving what is done to his Spirit, saying: "I was a stranger and you received me." Shall the poverty of many holy people, because it is unable to bring in wanderers and feed the hungry, be unkind and inhospitable to the Lord, who is accustomed to find his lodging with the poor by preference? . . . . "Upon whom," he says, shall I rest if not with the humble? "In all I sought rest, but I found it with a humble handmaid." No one was found like her in the grace of humility, therefore all the fullness of the godhead rested even in bodily form in this fullness of humility.[5]

It is to her, the perfect model of our hiddenness, that we turn each evening in the Salve Regina. Mary is the final word of every day of our lives.

O clemens,
O pia,
O dulcis, Virgo Maria!

---

[4] *Constitutions*, C. 45.1
[5] Guerric, *Sermo in assumptione BVM*, CF 32:182–183.

PSALMS IN THE NIGHT

He will not let your foot be moved;
he who keeps you will not slumber.
He who keeps Israel
will neither slumber nor sleep.
The Lord is your keeper;
the Lord is your shade at your right hand.
The sun shall not strike you by day,
nor the moon by night.

Psalm 121:3-6

In this essay I would like to comment more personally about my experience of what the psalmist calls "songs in the night."

> At night his song is with me,
> a prayer to the God of my life.[1]

In fact, it was on my bed at night that I was first drawn inside a psalm, not partly inside as often happens, or even deeply, but completely. The psalm was 63 and the particular words:

> My soul is satisfied as with a rich feast,
> and my mouth praises you with joyful lips
> when I think of you on my bed,
> and meditate on you in the watches of the night;
> for you have been my help,
> *AND IN THE SHADOW OF YOUR WINGS I SING FOR JOY!*[2]

This song of joy, more like a shout, came from a place so deep within that no explanation could ever suffice for it except that of Cassian's which I read many years later:

[1] Ps 42:8.
[2] Ps 63:5-7.

102

Thriving on the pasturage that they always offer and taking into himself all the dispositions of the psalms, he will begin to repeat them and to treat them in his profound compunction of heart not as if they were composed by the prophet but as if they were his own utterances and his own prayer. Certainly he will consider that they are directed to his own person, and he will recognize that their words were not only achieved by and in the prophet in times past but that they are daily borne out and fulfilled in him. For divine Scripture is clearer and its inmost organs, so to speak, are revealed to us when our experience not only perceives but even anticipates its thought, and the meanings of the words are disclosed to us not by exegesis but by proof. When we have the same disposition in our heart with which each psalm was sung or written down, then we shall become like its author, grasping its significance beforehand rather than afterward. . . . Having been instructed in this way, with our dispositions for our teachers, we shall grasp this as something seen rather than heard, and from the inner disposition of the heart we shall bring forth not what has been committed to memory but what is inborn in the very nature of things. Thus we shall penetrate its meaning not through the written text but with experience leading the way. So it is that our mind will arrive at that incorruptible prayer . . . that is not only not laid hold of by the sight of some image, but it cannot even be grasped by any word or phrase. Rather, once the mind's attentiveness has been set ablaze, it is called forth in an unspeakable ecstasy of heart and with an insatiable gladness of spirit.[3]

When a psalm verse issues from the heart with such unaccountable keenness of spirit, it remains etched on the soul forever as one's very own, as an original, as never before or since prayed this way. On that night long ago the Spirit of God cried out through my very bones and marrow, and his joy became my joy, if only for a second.

It was thus that I learned that the psalms belong to the night as well as to the day, to resting as well as to the Divine Office, to

---

[3] John Cassian, *The Conferences,* translated and annotated by Boniface Ramsey (New York: Paulist Press, 1997) 384–385.

less conscious moments as well as to our deliberate efforts at continual prayer. Years later as a novice here I experienced the inside of another psalm as I lay upon my bed, this time in very different interior circumstances. My inability to take in so much "wide open space of God" at one time or, to put it another way, my tendency to want to fill up the emptiness of this simple life pushed me into a state of existential anxiety, most recognizable by the knots in my stomach. When they started to show up at night, depriving me of much needed sleep, I became desperate. What to do? Since my novice director had been recommending the psalms as personal prayer, I tried one without anticipating in the least what would happen. I prayed Psalm 121:

> I lift up my eyes to the hills—
> from where will my help come?
> My help comes from the Lord,
> who made heaven and earth.
> He will not let your foot be moved;
> he who keeps you will not slumber.
> He who keeps Israel
> will neither slumber nor sleep.[4]

Rarely did I move beyond those words because every time I reached the question, "From where will my help come?" my soul turned a quiet gaze of hope to the Father. It was just a handful of hope during which my pain would ease, yet when I moved on to the next words my anxious feelings would overpower me again. Naturally I began to look forward to the question and to the momentary calm it brought, for it was always in one of those moments that I would fall off to sleep again. After several weeks I noticed that when I reached the question, the space of the calm would be more prolonged, enabling me to fall asleep more quickly. After several months, my hope and my trust had so grown through this dialogue in the night that I had only to say "I lift" and the calm would return, and so it has remained to this day. If we but knew the gifts of God!

His gift of gifts, the Holy Spirit, is at work in us by day and by night, and this you may have discovered when, upon wak-

---

[4] Ps 121:1-4.

ing some mornings, you are mysteriously aware of clearer light or deeper conviction. Once I went to bed wrestling with a decision I needed to make and feeling myself in a bind, much as I imagine Saint Joseph felt when faced with Mary's pregnancy. And then the words came to me that would remain my closest psalm friend for many years:

> I bless the Lord who gives me counsel;
> in the night also my heart instructs me.[5]

In those words I heard his voice guiding me into one course rather than another and the sound of his voice was unmistakable. It was the sound of a most quiet and most certain peace, quieter than the night.

One other experience of a psalm at night should be mentioned. It occurred before I entered and it involved the acute pain of feeling that God was no longer calling me to the contemplative/monastic life, that he had changed his mind. Through sleepless nights these words helped me to name that pain as grief:

> I think of God, and I moan;
> I meditate, and my spirit faints.
> You keep my eyelids from closing;
> I am so troubled that I cannot speak.
> I consider the days of old,
> and remember the years of long ago.
> I commune with my heart in the night;
> I meditate and search my spirit:
> "Will the Lord spurn for ever,
> and never again be favorable?
> Has his steadfast love ceased forever?
> Are his promises at an end for all time?
> Has God forgotten to be gracious?
> Has he in anger shut up his compassion?"
> And I say, "It is my grief
> that the right hand of the Most High has changed."[6]

[5] Ps 16:7.
[6] Ps 77:10.

These words, especially the last sentence, struck my heart like
an arrow, and consequently it is never without a joy as profound as my former grief that I pray Psalm 77, experiencing as I
have for so many years now that God never takes back his gifts
or revokes his choice, that is, that the right hand of the Most
High does not change.

And you, what have been your psalms in the night, psalms
your own heart has written in the Spirit?

PSALM 95: TODAY!

Come ring out our joy to the Lord;
hail the rock who saves us.
Let us come before him, giving thanks,
with songs let us hail the Lord.
A mighty God is the Lord,
a great king above all gods.
In his hand are the depths of the earth;
the heights of the mountains are his.
To him belongs the sea, for he made it
and the dry land shaped by his hands.
Come in; let us bow and bend low;
let us kneel before the God who made us
for he is our God and we
the people who belong to his pasture,
the flock that is led by his hand.
O that today you would listen to his voice!
Harden not your hearts as at Meribah,
as on that day at Massah in the desert
when your fathers put me to the test;
when they tried me, though they saw my work.
For forty years I was wearied of these people
and I said: "Their hearts are astray,
these people do not know my ways."
Then I took an oath in my anger:
"Never shall they enter my rest."[1]

Psalm 95 is the vigilatrix of our souls. Clearly, faithfully, and persuasively she calls to us in the fourth watch of the night,

[1] The Grail Psalter.

walks toward us on the sea of sleep: "Listen and adore, obey and bend low, for this is who you are."

Each day is a new creation, and he who holds the depths of the earth in his hands, holds us too. He gives us today; he gives us himself today. He renews with us the covenant in which we became his people and he our God.

"Come in, let us bow and bend low, let us kneel before the God who made us, for he is our God." If these words descend upon you like an overshadowing cloud, if they lead you within to that silent sanctuary where God is God, then let it be. Let the other words, the other calls of the psalm be muted in favor of this word of profound adoration for which you were created.

The Cistercian life is one of profound bows moving toward full prostration, and our souls are shaped by them. "Bow down" in Hebrew did not merely describe exterior posture but quickly came to be used for the inward religious attitude of prayer; thus it is often translated as "worship." First we go down on our knees, then place our hands on the ground, and finally descend to the dust, our faces to the earth. Something deep within us yearns to express our creaturehood fully by bending low before God; by yielding to the desire "to praise him at no less cost than that of the wild, perfect, supreme love that transcends every other love, every other work, every other desire, to lose itself entirely from the eyes of men in that profound abyss which is known as adoration."[2]

It is from this interior posture that we will be most receptive to the second call: "Oh that today you would listen to his voice! Harden not your hearts." Think of Moses at the burning bush who, removing his sandals and hiding his face, heard what had never before been heard—the name of God. True listening will always be like that: humble, reverent, bent low.

In Hebrew the word for "listen" or "hear" is *shema kol*, literally, "to listen to the voice," God's voice, a listening that is essentially heeding, obeying. In fact, it is the very verb for obeying. But we are so out of practice. Every morning we wake up with

---

[2] Thomas Merton, *The Waters of Siloe* (New York: Harcourt, Brace and Company, 1949) 264.

Massah and *Meribah,* our deep-set inclination to revolt. Happily, we also wake up with Jesus, the Servant who teaches us day by day the art of non-resistance to the Father's word:

> Morning by morning he wakens—
> wakens my ear
> to listen as those who are taught.
> The Lord God has opened my ear,
> and I was not rebellious,
> I did not turn backward.[3]

In him we continually observe what obedience really is, a listening so attuned to God's voice that his thoughts, words and deeds flow from that voice as from a pure spring: "I can do nothing on my own authority. As I hear, I judge; and my judgment is just, because I seek not my own will but the will of him who sent me."[4]

For the monk, this heedful listening to the voice, whether it comes directly or mediated, will always be the way into the depths of the life, into prayer, love, communion. Our fathers and mothers had a clear understanding of obedience as the key to the interior. When the psalmist says, "Never shall they (the disobedient) enter my rest," he refers primarily to the promised land; but in time "rest" came to mean the eternal sabbath:

> For if Joshua had given them rest, God would not speak later about another day. So then, a sabbath rest still remains for the people of God; for those who enter God's rest also cease from their labors as God did from his. Let us therefore make every effort to enter that rest, so that no one may fall through such disobedience as theirs.[5]

As I mentioned earlier, the theme of rest is very significant in monastic spirituality. *Requies,* eternal rest in God without whom our hearts are restless, was preceded this side of heaven by the experience of *quies,* which is stillness, interior prayer, repose in God; and the door to *quies* is obedience. As Saint Bernard teaches:

---

[3] Isa 50:4-5.
[4] John 5:30.
[5] Heb 4:8-11.

"From your precepts I learn wisdom" said the Psalmist, that you may know the grace of contemplation is never owed except to the commandments. Do not imagine that love of your own repose is to become an obstacle to the way of obedience and the traditions of the seniors. If so, the Bridegroom will not sleep in the same bed with you, especially if, instead of the flowers of obedience, you have bestrewn it with the hemlock and nettles of disobedience. Because of this he will not listen to your prayers. When you call he will not come. Nor will this great lover of obedience who preferred to die rather than disobey, put himself into the power of one who will not obey. He will not approve the empty repose of your contemplation.[6]

All this in a psalm; all this in a day! Come then, let us ring out our joy to the Lord for the gift of today, those spaces measured out so carefully by God to fit our human energy, those frequent new beginnings in which his call to adore and to listen gives us a fresh start in becoming ourselves. Let us come into his presence giving thanks for every day, "as long as it is called today."

[6] Bernard, *SC*, CF 7:244.

PSALM 103: UNIVERSAL TENDERNESS

Bless the Lord, my soul,
bless his holy name, all that is in me!
Bless the Lord, my soul,
and remember all his kindnesses:
in forgiving all your offences,
in curing all your diseases,
in redeeming your life from the pit,
in crowning you with love and tenderness,
in filling your years with prosperity,
in renewing your youth like an eagle's.
The Lord, who does what is right,
is always on the side of the oppressed;
he revealed his intentions to Moses,
his prowess to the people of Israel.
The Lord is tender and compassionate,
slow to anger, most loving;
his indignation does not last for ever,
his resentment exists a short time only;
he never treats us, never punishes us,
as our guilt and our sins deserve.
No less than the height of heaven over earth
is the greatness of his love for those who fear him;
he takes our sins farther away
than the east is from the west.
As tenderly as a father treats his children,
so the Lord treats those who fear him;
he knows of what we are made,
he remembers that we are dust.
As for mortals, their days are like grass;

they flourish like a flower of the field;
for the wind passes over it, and it is gone,
and its place knows it no more.
But the Lord's love for those who fear him
lasts from all eternity and for ever,
like his goodness to their children's children,
as long as they keep his covenant
and remember to obey his precepts.
The Lord has fixed his throne in the heavens,
his sovereign power rules over all.
Bless the Lord, all his angels,
mighty warriors who fulfill his commands,
attentive to the sound of his words.
Bless the Lord, all his armies,
servants who fulfill his wishes.
Bless the Lord, all his works,
in every place where he rules.
Bless the Lord, my soul.[1]

Open the door of this room slowly, softly. By the bed you
will see someone kneeling as he pours oil and wine on the
wounds of another, bandaging them carefully. Truly no psalm
captures God's tender care for the weak more than this one:

Bless the Lord, my soul,
and remember all his kindnesses:
in forgiving all your offences,
in curing all your diseases . . .
He knows of what we are made,
he remembers that we are dust.

This hymn of thanksgiving for God's steadfast love springs
from the revelation of himself to Moses on Sinai, and yet it transcends that revelation, probably due to so many more years of
experiencing the divine tenderness. Paralleled, the passages
look like this:

[1] Translation adapted to text.

Exodus 34:6-7	*Psalm 103:8-10*
The Lord, the Lord, a God of tenderness and compassion, slow to anger, rich in kindness and faithfulness; for thousands he maintains his kindness, forgives faults, transgression, sin; yet he lets nothing go unchecked, punishing the father's fault in the sons and in the grandsons to the third and fourth generation.	The Lord is tender and compassionate, slow to anger, most loving; his indignation does not last forever, his resentment exists a short time only; he never treats us, never punishes us, as our guilt and our sins deserve. . . . He takes our sins farther away than the east is from the west.

Let's look especially at the tenderness word, for in no other psalm does it have such a central place:

> Remember all his kindnesses . . . in crowning
> you with love and tenderness . . .
> The Lord is tender and compassionate . . .
> As tenderly as a father treats his children,
> so the Lord treats those who fear him.

God's tenderness, in Hebrew *rahamim*, is rooted in the word "womb" and is expressive of a love of a vulnerable nature; an infinite affection seen most clearly in the tenderness of a mother for her child. "Pity" and "compassion" are insufficient to convey the warmth and intimacy this word contains, for it witnesses better than any other to God's heartfelt yearning for us, a yearning expressed so poignantly by these words from the book of Hosea, the prophet of *rahamim:*

> Ephraim, how could I part with you?
> Israel, how could I give you up?[2]

The most beautiful thing about tenderness, no matter from what direction you view it, is its profound closeness to the heart of God, its innermost quality. Scripturally it has been described as the interior sentiment which is the source of *hesed,* God's steadfast love;[3] philosophically it has been described as the feeling

---

[2] Hos 11:8.

[3] Jacques Guillet, *Themes of the Bible* (Notre Dame, Indiana: Fides Publishers, Inc., 1960) 40.

component of compassion;[4] mystically it has been described as what is most divine in divine love.[5] When genuine tenderness touches our lives, we know that someone has felt with and for our whole person, has felt even our most "deeply hidden spiritual tremors," and has cared deeply for us. Tenderness has no reason apart from love,[6] and just as we know that God is love, we cannot doubt either that he is tenderness.

In our own tradition Saint Gertrud became the herald of the Divine Tenderness, in Latin *Pietas,* and proclaimed indefatigably God's desire that we place absolute trust in his tender love for us. She herself grew more and more in the image of this tender God as her biographer tells us: "It was not only toward people but toward every creature that she experienced so strong a feeling of loving-kindness *(pietas);* if she saw any creature, bird or animal, suffering distress from hunger or thirst or cold, from the depths of her loving heart she immediately felt compassion for the Lord's handiwork."[7] What we glimpse here is the total transformation of a person in Christ, even to the evangelization of the passions and emotions.

We find in Saint Aelred a passage which illustrates well this gradual transformation. When he speaks of the sabbath of fraternal charity, he shows us the expansion of the heart in six stages: our blood relatives, our friends, our community members, all Christians, those outside the Church, and, finally, our enemies: "What trouble, what disturbance, what grief, what anxiety can tarnish the joy of someone who, from that first sabbath . . . progresses by a fuller grace to the state of divine likeness? There, embracing the whole human race in the one love of his mind, he is not troubled by any injury from anyone. Rather, just as a fond father has a tender affection for a dearly-beloved

---

[4] Karol Wojtyla, *Love and Responsibility* (New York: Farrar, Straus, Giroux, 1981) 201–202.

[5] Olivier Quenardel, Abbot of Citeaux, from a talk on Saint Gertrud addressed to those attending the Institute of Cistercian Patrimony at Citeaux, October 1997.

[6] See Wojtyla, *Love and Responsibility,* 204, 207.

[7] Gertrud, *Herald,* CF 35:62.

son suffering delirium, so likewise will he not think unkindly of his enemies."[8]

> As tenderly as a Father treats his children . . .

Truly we are meant to become compassionate and tender-hearted as our Father is compassionate and tenderhearted. As we bless the Lord for all his kindnesses we ourselves become kinder, and our hearts begin to yearn to be filled with what the spiritual tradition of the Eastern Churches has so fittingly called, "universal tenderness." May she in whom there is "nothing austere, nothing to terrify,"[9] the one who was "pregnant with inexhaustible tenderness,"[10] keep us on this path until we, too, become tender and compassionate, slow to anger, most loving, and, as Benedict says, humbly patient with human weakness.[11] For God knows of what we are made.

[8] Aelred of Rievaulx, *Mirror of Charity*. Cistercian Fathers series 17 (Kalamazoo: Cistercian Publications, 1990) 227–229.

[9] Bernard of Clairvaux, *Sermo dominica infra octavam assumptionis*, *St. Bernard's Sermons for the Seasons and Principal Festivals of the Year*, vol. III, (Dublin: Browne and Nolan, Limited, 1925) 259.

[10] Guerric, *Asspt*, CF 32:169.

[11] RB 72:5.

PSALM 119
AND THE RULE OF SAINT BENEDICT

Oh, how I love your law!
It is my meditation all day long.
Your commandment makes me wiser than my enemies,
for it is always with me.
I have more understanding than all my teachers,
for your decrees are my meditation.
I understand more than the aged,
for I keep your precepts.
I hold back my feet from every evil way,
in order to keep your word.
I do not turn away from your ordinances,
for you have taught me.
How sweet are your words to my taste,
sweeter than honey to my mouth!
Through your precepts I get understanding;
therefore I hate every false way.
                              Psalm 119:97-104

Now we approach Psalm 119, the largest room in the house and the one in which the psalmist exclaims in myriad ways one blessed message: "God has spoken to us!" Again and again he echoes Israel's profound gratitude for and intoxication with the word:

> For ask now about former ages, long before your own, ever since the day that God created human beings on the earth; ask from one end of heaven to the other: has any-thing so great as this ever happened or has its like ever

been heard of? Has any people ever heard the voice of a god speaking out of a fire, as you have heard, and lived?[1]

Upon opening the door, do not be surprised to find Saint Benedict within, for our Father spent so much of his time in this room that we can see it in the very structure of his Rule. Let's consider this under the following themes: journey, humility, and praise.

THE JOURNEY TO GOD

"Truly as we advance in this way of life and faith, our hearts open wide, and we run with unspeakable sweetness of love on the path of God's commandments."[2] In this passage at the conclusion of his Prologue, a passage in which Benedict significantly departs from the Rule of the Master to reveal to us his heart with all its depths of wisdom, desire, and fatherly solicitude, we meet our first allusion to Psalm 119: "I run the way of your commandments, for you enlarge my heart." This beautiful statement of Benedict is the climax of several that depict the monk as one with a journey to make: "Return to him . . . Follow him to glory . . . The Lord shows us the path to life . . . Let us walk in his paths . . . If we would arrive . . . Do not fly from the path of salvation whose beginning must be narrow."

We are on a journey from fear to love, death to life, unlikeness to likeness, and it is urgent that we neither depart nor detour from this path so that we may arrive speedily at our destination. What manner of travel best assures this? Benedict says "Run!" In fact, he says it four times in the Prologue, even changing Saint John's "walk" to "run":

Run *(currite)* while you have the light of life.[3]

We shall not dwell in it unless we run *(currendo)* by our good deeds.[4]

---

[1] Deut 4:32-33.
[2] RB Prologue:49; Ps 119:32.
[3] RB Prologue:13.
[4] RB Prologue:22.

We must hasten *(currendum)* to do now what will profit us for all eternity.[5]

We shall run *(curritur)* in the ways of God's commandments.[6]

Running toward a goal takes one's entire attention and all one's energy. It is a sign of tremendous eagerness and desire, for one strains forward looking to neither left nor right. No comparisons, no diversions. This theme will continue throughout the Rule. The disciple of Benedict runs to the Work of God at the rising bell and every bell. She runs to obey the voice of her superiors (the speedy step of obedience), going so swiftly in fact that the command and its fulfillment are practically simultaneous—"At the hearing of the ear he obeyed me." In the person of the portress, she hastens to every charitable service. Her attitude is always to anticipate the other in honor. She is a person who knows where she is going and goes there. There is a deep and abiding sense of purpose about a true monk. This does not mean that what she does is done hurriedly. It means that everything she does is so directly a response to God, so clearly a straight way to her Creator, that what she does and the spirit in which she does it is itself the "running" to which Saint Benedict refers.

Only love can make us run like this, a love full of desire. Though external circumstances may remain narrow, the heart becomes wide by clearing the land of all that would impede the steps of the Lord of Glory. As Saint Bernard writes:

What can I say of her who can provide avenues spacious enough for the God of majesty to walk in! She certainly cannot afford to be entangled in law-suits nor by worldly cares; she cannot be enslaved by gluttony and sensual pleasures, by the lust of the eyes, the ambition to rule, or by pride in the possession of power. If she is to become heaven, the dwelling place of God, it is first of all essential that she be empty of all these defects. Otherwise how could she be still enough to know that he is God? Nor may she yield in the least to hatred or envy or bitterness, "be-

[5] RB Prologue:44.
[6] RB Prologue:49.

cause wisdom will not enter a deceitful soul." The soul must grow and expand, that it may be roomy enough for God. Its width is its love, if we accept what the Apostle says: "Widen your hearts in love."[7]

This divine love, then, that expands the heart with an unspeakable sweetness, has a momentum of its own. This love either stretches forward to or flows onward from a crucial milestone in the life of the monk: the irrevocable commitment of monastic profession, a ceremony in which Psalm 119 has been sung by every monk for fifteen hundred years in an unforgettable moment: "Receive me, O Lord, as you have promised and I shall live; do not disappoint me in my hope."[8] So sings the novice three times, repeated each time by the community. Then the novice prostrates herself at the feet of all that they may pray for her, and from that day on she is considered part of the community.

This blessed hope of which she sings and dreams and casts her whole future on, is no ephemeral thing, for God does not faint or grow weary and "those who wait for the Lord shall renew their strength; they shall mount up with wings like eagles; they shall run and not be weary!"[9]

HUMILITY

It is good for me that you have humbled me that I may learn your commandments.[10]

I am bent down and humbled in every way.[11]

The first of these passages from Psalm 119 is in the seventh degree of humility, the ultimate interior step; the second is in the twelfth, the ultimate exterior expression. Let's consider both of them in turn.

Some speak of the seventh step of humility as the top of the ladder, the peak, but I prefer to think of it as the ultimate depth of the process. Picture Jesus, our model, descending the steps of

---

[7] Bernard, *SC*, CF 7:83.
[8] RB 58:21; Ps 119:116.
[9] Isa 40:31.
[10] Ps 119:71, 73; RB 7:54.
[11] Ps 119:107; RB 7:66.

humility to become obedient even unto death. Just as that magnificent hymn Philippians 2 follows a descending movement, so too do Benedict's steps of humility:

> obedience to the Father
>   to obedience to others out of love for the Father
>   to obedience in difficulties and even injustice
>   to joy in the poorest and the worst
>   to heartfelt inner conviction of one's absolute
>   poverty before God.

We see that this path of humble yielding leads to the lowest and deepest place of all, the interiority of the human heart where the understanding is illumined ("you have humbled me that I may learn") and where, with the deepest conviction, we can exclaim with the psalmist, "I have chosen the way of truth."[12] Here it is that wisdom is born, the wisdom of humility.

In the twelfth step, the humility which fills the inmost heart of the monk has permeated her very body: "I am bent down and humbled in every way." In the first step she is ever attentive to God and always on her guard against sin; in this final step she has a new rapport with the sinner and actually looks like the humble publican with head inclined. But beneath and beyond this is the image of Jesus bowing his head on the cross in the moment of his deepest humility:

> He let himself be taken for a sinner.[13]

One cannot imitate the humble stance, the bent head. It is the heart that is bent low that radiates from within. Recall the beautiful saying about Saint Anthony who was visited each year by three fathers, one of whom always remained silent. After a long time Abba Anthony said to him, "You often come here to see me, but you never ask me anything," and the other replied, "It is enough for me to see you, Father."[14] Yes, those who are possessed by the twelfth step of humility speak to us without a word.

[12] Ps 119:30.
[13] Isa 53:12.
[14] *The Sayings*, CS 59:6.

PRAISE

Nothing so affects the structure of the Rule as praise. "Seven times a day I praise you,"[15] seven being the sacred and complete number. The truest sense of this verse of Psalm 119 is that the psalmist is totally God's and his disposition is a continual state of adoration. Saint Benedict gives the verse a more literal incarnation so that within each day of prayer, the times of communal worship become the precious moments, the milestones so to speak, in which all the moments of prayer are gathered up. These moments are recapitulations, not interruptions, which reintensify our efforts at continual prayer and, beyond that, immerse us again and again in the prayer of Christ who never ceases to intercede for us and for the whole human race.

RB 16 is a field in which two treasures are buried, both of them verses from Psalm 119 which have shaped the hearts of monks for centuries. One is "Seven times a day"[16] and the other "In the middle of the night I rise to praise you"[17] or, in Latin, *Media nocte surgebam ad confitendum tibi.* No monk can hear *Media nocte* ("in the middle of the night") without hearing more than Psalm 119, for the resonance is strong and carries the Good News of the coming of the Bridegroom. "At midnight there was a cry, 'The Bridegroom is here! Go out and meet him.' At this, all those bridesmaids woke up and trimmed their lamps."[18] Suddenly we are within the pure praise of Christ in his eschatological kingdom. This is the blessed mystery contained in the psalms and in all Scripture: they feed us, yet forever point to the One who alone can satisfy, Jesus. He is the word that we eat and drink and pant for; that we commit our lives to, run toward, hope in, die in. "Whoever drinks this wine of Scripture hunts for Jesus and finds him, reaching him on the wooded heights."[19]

---

[15] Ps 119:164.
[16] RB 16:1, 3.
[17] RB 16:4-5; Ps 119:62.
[18] Matt 25:5-7.
[19] Henri de Lubac, *Medieval Exegesis*, volume 1 (Grand Rapids: William B. Eerdmans Publishing Company, 1998) 3.

How can we respond worthily to the thorough formation this psalm provides in our monastic lives? One verse says it:

> Oh, how I love your law!
> It is my meditation all day long.[20]

---

[20] Ps 119:97.

THE GRADUAL PSALMS

How very good and pleasant it is
when kindred live together in unity!
It is like the precious oil on the head,
running down upon the beard,
on the beard of Aaron,
running down over the collar of his robes.
It is like the dew of Hermon,
which falls on the mountains of Zion.
For there the Lord ordained his blessing,
life forevermore.

Psalm 133

Saint Benedict chose the gradual psalms for frequent use and, like household vessels for everyday, their very frequency makes them familiar and dear. They are songs of "we," of a people, a family, a community journeying together, ascending together, sharing life with all its frictions and joys. Even when the "I" surfaces, the "we" or "us" is not far behind. Naturally, then, Jesus enters into our experience of them as head of his body, as the first among many brothers and sisters, as one gladly receiving a cup of water from another.

These psalms ascend toward a great peak: Jerusalem. And the Rule of Saint Benedict, too, ascends toward a great peak, that of "most fervent love" as described in chapter 72. Ultimately these two peaks are one and the same, for what is the heavenly Jerusalem if not the fullness of love? One phrase in particular, "may he bring us all together" captures the spiritual affinity between the ascent in the Rule and the ascent in the gradual psalms, so let us consider these psalms in the light of Saint Benedict's teaching on mutual charity.

First of all the spirit of social stability so evident in these psalms is not a human creation but something grounded in faith and trust in the God who gathers us together in Christ:

> Those who trust in the Lord are like Mount Zion
> which cannot be moved, but abides forever.
> As the mountains surround Jerusalem,
> so the Lord surrounds his people,
> from this time on and forevermore.[1]

This particular psalm was my daily Tierce friend for many years. I would enter within it and assert boldly: "I trust. Therefore I cannot be moved from this monastic people. I am as surely theirs as my feet are standing on this ground!" Fixed firmly in our purpose, we pray together, labor together, and go on no matter what.

There is no joy like praying together. Spontaneously we sing with the psalmist:

> I rejoiced when I heard them say,
> "Let us go to God's house."
> And now our feet are standing
> within your gates, O Jerusalem . . .
> For Israel's law it is
> there to praise the Lord's name.[2]

This ardent joy is captured in the traditional Cistercian hymn for Tierce in which we can easily imagine not only song but also the heart's fire darting from choir to choir antiphonally:

> May mind, with mouth and tongue,
> Each sense and every power,
> Be prompt in praise, aflame with love,
> To kindle all we meet.

Was William of Saint Thierry thinking of this when he wrote these words?

---

[1] Ps 125:1-2.
[2] Ps 122:1-2, 4 (The Grail Psalter).

There is such a dutiful, such a harmonious, such a fervent melody of psalms that they appear to present before, and sacrifice to God a song of life, of manners, of a good *affectus,* well composed according to a sort of harmony not of music but of the rule of charity. In the common exercises of piety, in that grace from the faces and in the bodies and dispositions, they see in one another the presence of the divine goodness and are surrounded with so great an *affectus* that, like the Seraphim, one catches fire from another in the love of God, nor can anyone give another enough to suit himself.[3]

Working together, too, with its rhythms of toil, rest, difficulty, and success, affords deep human satisfaction when it is done humanly, that is, when it aims to make life more human.[4] The images in the gradual psalms witness to this healthy attitude.

Those who go out weeping,
bearing the seed for sowing,
shall come home with shouts of joy,
carrying their sheaves.[5]

It is in vain that you rise up early
and go late to rest,
eating the bread of anxious toil;
for he gives sleep to his beloved.[6]

You shall eat the fruit of the labor of your hands;
you shall be happy, and it shall go well with you.[7]

Best of all the work descriptions is the good zeal, the joyful energy of David who vowed "not to enter tent or house, not to climb into bed, not to allow himself sleep, not even to close his eyes, until he had found a place for the Lord, a home for the Mighty One of Jacob!"[8] To labor like this in order to build up the

[3] William, *Nat am,* CF 30:84-85.
[4] John Paul II, Encyclical Letter *On Human Work* (Rome, 1981) number 3.
[5] Ps 126:6.
[6] Ps 127:2.
[7] Ps 128:2.
[8] Ps 132: 3-5.

Body where God dwells in the Spirit is truly to love with all one's strength. It is that most fervent love that considers not what is useful for oneself but what benefits the other, the love our fathers and mothers so frequently encouraged within community.

> Let this, then, my brothers, be the model of your life; for such is the rule of holy living: with Christ, to live in thought and desire in our eternal country; for Christ, to refuse no service of charity in this harsh earthly existence. In imitation of Christ, to ascend to the Father, letting oneself be calmed, simplified, and unified in restful meditation; in imitation of Christ, to descend to one's brothers, letting oneself be distended, torn, shared, divided, becoming all in action.[9]

This life of fidelity to one another in prayer and work, in simple things as well as great, is so good and so joyful. The recent document "Fraternal Life in Community" speaks of this joy and ends with a citation from a precious gradual psalm:

> We must not forget in the end that peace and pleasure in being together are among the signs of the kingdom of God. The joy of living even in the midst of difficulties along the human and spiritual path and in the midst of daily annoyances is already part of the kingdom. This joy is a fruit of the Spirit and embraces the simplicity of existence and monotonous texture of daily life. A joyless fraternity is one that is dying out; before long members will be tempted to seek elsewhere what they can no longer find within their own home. A fraternity rich in joy is a genuine gift from above to brothers and sisters who know how to ask for it and to accept one another, committing themselves to fraternal life, trusting in the action of the Spirit. Thus the words of the psalm are made true: "Behold how good and pleasant it is when brothers dwell in unity . . . For there the Lord has commanded his blessing, life for evermore."[10]

---

[9] Isaac of Stella, from Sermon 12 as quoted in *Christian Readings*, Volume III, Year I (New York: Catholic Book Publishing Co., 1972) 27. See also Isaac of Stella, *Sermons on the Christian Year*. Cistercian Fathers series 11 (Kalamazoo: Cistercian Publications, 1979) 101.

[10] *Fraternal Life in Community* (Rome: Congregation for Institutes of Consecrated Life and Societies of Apostolic Life, 1994) number 28.

Let us sing the gradual psalms in this spirit, that is, in gratitude for the simple joys of our everyday life together. Let us delight in our interdependence in Christ as the branches of the vine and the shoots round the olive tree.

PSALM 147: A MIRROR FOR NOVICES

Praise the Lord, O Jerusalem!
Praise your God, O Zion!
For he strengthens the bars of your gates;
he blesses your children within you.
He grants peace within your borders;
he fills you with the finest of wheat.
He sends out his command to the earth;
his word runs swiftly.
He gives snow like wool;
he scatters frost like ashes.
He hurls down hail like crumbs—
who can stand before his cold?
He sends out his word, and melts them;
he makes his wind blow, and the waters flow.
He declares his word to Jacob,
his statutes and ordinances to Israel.
He has not dealt thus with any other nation;
they do not know his ordinances.
Praise the Lord!

Psalm 147:12-20

As we saw earlier, one of the graces of the psalms is that they serve as a mirror for the movements of the human soul, both the beautiful and the perverse. Within the same context, Saint Athanasius also states that "Whatever your particular need or trouble, from this same book you can select a form of words to fit it so that you do not merely hear and then pass on, but learn the way to remedy your ill."[1]

---

[1] Athanasius, *Epistola ad Marcellinum*, 103.

Psalm 147 contains some words that Bernard, the novice, looked into and, looking, immediately recognized his condition: "Who can stand before his cold?"

> I am not ashamed to admit that very often I myself, especially in the early days of my conversion experienced coldness and hardness of heart, while deep in my being I sought for him whom I longed to love. I could not yet love him since I had not yet really found him; at best my love was less than it should have been, and for that very reason I sought to increase it, for I would not have sought him if I did not already love him in some degree. I sought him therefore that in him my numbed and languid spirit might find warmth and repose, for nowhere could I find a friend to help me, whose love would thaw the wintry cold that chilled my inward being, and bring back again the feeling of spring-like bliss and spiritual delight. But my languor and weariness only increased, my soul melted away for sorrow, even to the verge of despair. All I could do was repeat softly to myself: "Who can stand before your cold?"[2]

In fact, years later at Clairvaux he would place his own novices before the same mirror. Yes, there is for beginners in the Cistercian way the danger of cold, even to the point of numbness, perhaps what we would call today culture shock.

> Do you see these novices? They came recently, they were converted recently. We cannot say of them that "our vineyard has flowered": it is flowering. What you see in them at the moment is the blossom; the time of fruiting has not yet come . . . For you, my young sons, I do not fear the cunning of the foxes, who are known to hunger for the fruits, not for the blossoms. The threat to you is from elsewhere. What I dread for the blossoms is not theft but blight from the cold. The north wind is unwelcome to me, and the morning frosts that are wont to destroy the early blossoms and deprive us of fruit. Hence any harm to you threatens from the north. "Who will endure your cold?"[3]

[2] Bernard, *SC*, CF 4:102.
[3] Bernard, *SC*, CF 31:166–167.

The cold is inevitable, shivering novices. The important thing is to find out how the natives of this strange land keep warm. Psalm 147 itself provides an answer that Bernard is not slow to detect: our communion in Christ with the mediation this involves is the secret of warmth and life. The Cistercian novice enters a community of peace and praise sustained by word and Eucharist, enters the sacrament of the Church incarnated in this particular monastic church:

> Praise the Lord, O Jerusalem!
> Praise your God, O Zion!
> For he strengthens the bars of your gates;
> he blesses your children within you.
> He grants peace within your borders;
> he fills you with the finest of wheat.
> He sends out his command to the earth;
> his word runs swiftly.

She experiences with the whole Body the alternate rhythms of God's blessing, although at the beginning she is likely to have a larger share of interior winter:

> He hurls down hail like crumbs—
> who can stand before his cold?
> He sends out his word, and melts them;
> he makes his wind blow, and the waters flow.

One good reason for this is that it grounds the beginner in humble, grateful receptivity to others and allows her to taste the truth that in Christ we all serve as instruments of God's saving grace to one another. Thus Bernard declares that warmth came to him as a novice not primarily through prayer but through the love and example of others:

> Then, at times when I least expected, at the word or even the sight of a good and holy man, at the memory of a dead or absent friend, he set his wind blowing and the waters flowing and my tears were my food day and night. How can I explain this? Only by ascribing it to the odor from the oil that anointed the friend in question. For me there was no anointing but rather the experience that came by an-

other's mediation . . . Many of you too, I feel, have had similar experiences, and have them even still. In what light then must we view them? I hold that through them our pride is shown up, our humility guarded, brotherly love fostered and good desires aroused.[4]

For us cenobites in the desert, such a narrow and wintry entrance is no accident but a sign of God's gracious wisdom as he leads us from fear to love by means of humility. Praise the Lord, Jerusalem!

---

[4] Bernard, *SC*, CF 4:102–103.

PSALM 148:
LET EARTH PRAISE THE LORD

Alleluia!
Let heaven praise the Lord:
praise him, heavenly heights!
Praise him, all his angels,
praise him, all his armies!
Praise him, sun and moon,
praise him, shining stars,
praise him, highest heavens,
and waters above the heavens!
Let them all praise the name of the Lord,
at whose command they were created.
He has fixed them in their place for ever,
by an unalterable statute.
Let earth praise the Lord:
sea monsters and all the deeps,
fire and hail, snow and mist,
gales that obey his decree,
mountains and hills,
orchards and forests,
wild animals and farm animals,
snakes and birds,
all kings on earth and nations,
princes, all rulers in the world,
young men and girls,
old people and children too!
Let them all praise the name of the Lord,
for his name and no other is sublime,
transcending earth and heaven in majesty,
raising the fortunes of his people,

> *to the praises of the devout,*
> *of Israel, the people dear to him.*[1]

Cistercians have always loved the desert, that is, the solitude of space. Whatever that space, whether it takes the shape of immense corn fields, hilly deserts, mountains, sea, or woods, we find that it both shapes us and sings in us. Psalm 148, which we pray at sunrise, is a most exuberant witness of this creaturely praise.

Let me enter this psalm through the perspective I know best, through this Wrentham, Massachusetts, space where, at all seasons the woods are dark and deep and lovely, woods from which a light beckons that I would hesitate to call divine, yet how close to the color of angels.

> Praise him, all his angels!

Take a day, any day, and walk in. If winter, you will touch the heart of Cistercian simplicity. Trees, unadorned, silent, stretching together to the sky, teach us an uncomplicated way to God.[2]

> Praise him, snow . . .
> Forests, praise him.

If fall, you will ache from so much beauty, especially fire. If early spring you may meet your first snake of the year, skinny black snakes who do no evil. But if late spring, the hermit thrush returns and with him, if he chooses to reveal his shy self, endless possibilities of consolation amid desolation, of depths calling to depths, of music unsurpassable. In my hardest times, the little hermit was always there, seemingly waiting to commune with me and to sing me a song from another world. He never failed.

> Praise him, snakes and birds.

Upon leaving the woods, return by the road behind the orchard, the one that passes the field beyond the vegetable garden.

---

[1] Translation adapted to text.
[2] *Constitutions.* See C. 27 on Simplicity.

New England fields are soft, somewhat small, and rarely complete without clouds. Sheep and lambs and llama graze quietly, well protected from the lonely coyotes who have invaded our parts. All are gifts. All are made for praising.

> Let earth praise the Lord . . .
> orchards and forests,
> wild animals and farm animals.

And whenever you have the chance, go to the apple orchard across the road and to the three meadows above it. You may find yourself longing for the inner meadow as much as Anthony did for the inner mountain.[3] Whatever the monk's space, it contains many loving surprises and revelations from the Lord and within it, just as within prayer, each will find a secret path with secret joys. These are the joys we bring each morning to the altar of Lauds, offering our praise and thanks to the Lord for and with all his creatures.

> Young men and girls,
> old people and children too!
> Let them all praise the name of the Lord,
> for his name and no other is sublime.

[3] See Athanasius, *The Life of Saint Anthony* (New York: Newman Press, 1978) 61–63.

ACKNOWLEDGMENTS

The Scripture quotations contained herein are from the New Revised Standard Version Bible, copyright © 1989 by the Division of Christian Education of the National Council of the Churches of Christ in the U.S.A., and are used by permission. All rights reserved.

A few psalms are quoted from The Grail, copyright © 1963, as they appear in *The Psalms,* a Deus Book edition of the Paulist Press, 1968 by special arrangement with Wm. Collins Sons & Co., Ltd. They are used with the permission of GIA/Gregorian Institute of America, Chicago, Illinois.

I wish to express my sincere thanks to all who have helped and encouraged me in the writing of this book, most particularly to the Wrentham novices whose enthusiasm in Psalm class, year after year, fired my own.

INDEX